St Lucia

DIRECTIONS

WRITTEN AND RESEARCHED BY

Natalie Folster and Karl Luntta

NEW YORK • LONDON • DELHI

www.roughguides.com

Contents

Introduction to

St Lucia

St Lucia lives up to the ideal of a Caribbean paradise, not least for its glorious array of honey-coloured and black volcanic sand beaches, translucent turquoise waters and sheltering reefs swarming

▲ Selling bananas at sea

with vibrant tropical fish. Despite development that has taken place over the past decade – which has resulted in some top-notch facilities – the island's feel remains decidedly laid-back, with little of the jaded hustle that can mar more established Caribbean destinations. It all makes for a relaxed, friendly and incredibly beautiful place to visit.

▲ Plantation

Archetypal beaches are in greatest number in the north, but to get the most out of the island, you're well advised to venture beyond built-up Rodney Bay and into the rugged wilderness of the east coast – defined by its crashing Atlantic surf, teeming nature reserves and lush botanical gardens – or the slow-paced fishing villages of the south, where brightly painted wooden boats line the bays. As a complement to any water-based activities you might indulge in – snorkelling, swimming,

When to visit

St Lucia's tropical climate is classically Caribbean. During **high season** (Dec–April), the island is pleasantly hot, with little rain and constant north-easterly trade winds that keep the nights cool. Temperatures rise even further during the **summer months**, which can also be wet: the rainy season lasts from June to October, with the **hurricane season** at the tail end, roughly from late August to October.

▲ Anse La Raye

deep-sea fishing – the pristine central interior region boasts all manner of hiking trails, found within protected forest reserves only populated by wildlife; the dramatic mountainous peaks of the Pitons lie to the southwest.

Even with these natural assets, St Lucia has only recently begun to attract visitors in any real number: as banana exports – long the mainstay of St Lucia's economy – plummeted in the late 1990s, the government intensified efforts to develop tourism. A clutch of luxury resorts opened on the southwest coast, but the island caters to all tastes: choose between upscale hotels or intimate guesthouses, dine in world-class restaurants or at roadside kiosks and shop in duty-free malls or at open-air village markets.

▼ Cas-en-Bas Beach

In the face of modernization, contemporary St Lucian culture has remained relatively unchanged, an amalgamation of the various customs, languages and traditions that have taken root here over the centuries. The warlike Caribs, who succeeded the Arawaks and Ciboney before them, ruled the island until being driven away by slave-owning Europeans in the seventeenth century, and

▲ Marjorie's Restaurant and Bar, Cas-en-Bas

evidence of St Lucia's layered past can be found in everything from Amerindian petroglyphs near Vieux Fort to the military ruins of Fort Charlotte in the north. African traditions involving magic and spiritualism survive in celebrations like summertime Carnival, and many islanders speak St Lucian Creole (a French patois), which evolved out of a common language used between French planters and their slaves. A similar blend is fortuitously found in Creole cuisine, which mixes spicy, tomato-based sauces and starchy carbohydrates of African and West Indian cooking with inventive garnishes more typical of French fare.

▲ Fishing boat on the west coast

St Lucia
AT A GLANCE

Castries and around

The bustling capital city of Castries – the island's centre of commerce and government – is home to half of St Lucia's population. Its few attractions include a lively central market and duty-free shopping malls, plus long strands of beach that lie north of town.

▼ Castries

Rodney Bay and Gros Islet

Rodney Bay is the hub of St Lucia's tourist activities, and a strip of restaurants, hotels and bars backs the thick swath of golden sand at the area's popular Reduit Beach. Nearby, the quiet

▼ Rodney Bay Marina

fishing village of Gros Islet hosts the wildly popular Friday night Jump Up street party.

The northern tip and the northeast coast

St Lucia's hilly northern tip is home to the residential community of Cap Estate, known for its luxurious hilltop villas, golf course and small resorts. It's a vivid contrast to the remote beaches that dot the wild Atlantic coast, which stretches from Pointe Hardy down to the long, lonesome sand at Grand Anse.

▼ Cap Estate

The central interior

Mountains, rainforest, cloud forest and elphin woodland cover St Lucia's central interior region. Its vast, uninhabited forest reserves offer numerous hiking trails boasting arresting scenery accented by exotic flora and fauna.

▲ Anse La Raye

The west coast

The winding west coast road running south from Castries is spectacularly scenic, passing by pretty Marigot Bay with its palm-fringed beach and through acres of banana plantations. A few secluded resorts are tucked along the way, good for quiet retreats.

▲ Soufrière

Soufrière and the Pitons

The twin peaks of the Pitons dominate St Lucia's southwest coast and loom over the old town of Soufrière, filled with narrow streets and balconied wooden houses. Waterfalls, botanical gardens, hiking trails and good diving and snorkelling spots make up the area's numerous natural attractions.

The south coast

Best appreciated for its scenery, the rural south coast between Soufrière and Vieux Fort is veined with rivers, waterfalls and velvety green ridges.

The east coast

A smattering of coastal fishing villages lines the largely undeveloped east coast; they may lack noteworthy hotels but that's sort of the point. Meanwhile, a string of stunning nature reserves protects St Lucia's teeming birdlife and delicate coastal ecology.

▼ Dennery

Ideas

The big six

The Caribbean island of St Lucia is endowed with spectacular natural scenery and a varied geography. There are iconic mountain peaks; lush, uninhabited rainforests; waters teeming with marine life; remnants of a violent colonial past, evocative and picturesque in their ruin; and plenty of postcard-perfect beaches on which to while away the day. The six sights listed here offer an overview of St Lucia's most compelling attractions.

▲ The rainforest

Though largely uninhabited and unmarked by roads, St Lucia's lush and mountainous rainforest is crisscrossed by scenic hiking trails.

P.134 ▶ THE CENTRAL INTERIOR

▲ The Pitons

The breathtaking peaks of Petit and Gros Piton, which rise out of the sea, are St Lucia's most photographed feature.

P.106 ▶ SOUFRIÈRE AND THE PITONS

▲ St Lucia's beaches

Laze away the day on the island's few dozen stretches of volcanic or coral sand – from popular Reduit Beach to the honey-coloured curve of Choc Beach to the secluded shores of Cas-en-Bas.

P.59 & P.69 ▶ CASTRIES & RODNEY BAY AND GROS ISLET

▼ Undersea life

The waters surrounding St Lucia hold pristine reefs ablaze with colour; deep underwater walls; and an abundance of sea creatures including whales, dolphins and brightly coloured fish.

P.102 ▶ SOUFRIÈRE AND THE PITONS

▼ Pigeon Island

Once a pirate hideout, then an eighteenth-century British fort, today Pigeon Island is a well-preserved historical site offering relaxing beaches, scenic hiking trails and stunning views.

P.70 ▶ RODNEY BAY AND GROS ISLET

▼ Marigot Bay

One of the prettiest bays in the Caribbean, with turquoise water fringed by light sand, palm trees and steep green hills dotted with elegant hotels.

P.90 ▶ THE WEST COAST

Beaches

St Lucia is rimmed with dozens of soft sandy beaches. Some are well-established relaxation spots, appointed with lounging chairs, shade umbrellas and bar service, while others are more rugged. The long Atlantic coast is pounded by a thundering surf and edged with miles of lonesome beaches, worth visiting for their dramatic vistas and privacy; the West Coast is washed by the gentler Caribbean Sea and is dotted with quiet coves suitable for swimming and snorkelling.

▲ Smuggler's Cove

A pretty, sheltered cove backed by tall cliffs and handy to Rodney Bay, minus the crowds of Reduit Beach.

P.82 ▸ THE NORTHERN TIP AND THE NORTHEAST COAST

▼ Anse de Sables

While the long, windswept stretch of blond sand here is favoured by windsurfers, it's otherwise hardly used – making it a good place for a stroll and a swim.

P.121 ▸ THE SOUTH COAST

▲ Anse Chastanet

One of the most attractive swimming beaches on the island and a top-notch luxury resort make this a popular vacation spot.

P.102 ▶ SOUFRIÈRE AND THE PITONS

▼ Reduit Beach

Enjoy watersports and people-watching at the island's most visited strip of sand.

P.69 ▶ RODNEY BAY AND GROS ISLET

◀ Anse Cochon

This secluded sweep of tawny sand on the west coast fronts a romantic clifftop resort and is a good place for snorkelling.

P.94 ▶ THE WEST COAST

Hikes

Hiking St Lucia's many trails is a good way to explore the island's landscape and see some unique flora and fauna. There are enough trails to fill a week or two, and options range from steep mountain treks to easy jaunts through the woods or along coastal paths. Many hiking paths lead to picturesque waterfalls, where you can cool off in clear mountain water.

▼ Piton Flore Trail

This strenuous 10km hike takes you up and over the summit of Piton Flore.

P.141 ▶ THE CENTRAL INTERIOR

▼ Saltibus Valley Trail

Follow a meandering mountain stream to a lacy, bracing waterfall.

P.118 ▶ THE SOUTH COAST

▲ Barre de L'Isle Trail

You might spot a boa constrictor or a mongoose while trekking the Barre de L'Isle, whose trailhead is only a short drive from Rodney Bay.

P.136 ▶ THE CENTRAL INTERIOR

▶ Millet Bird Sanctuary

A scenic 3km loop trail affords views of the island's rainforest, as well as a chance to spot five bird species found only on St Lucia.

P.92 ▶ THE WEST COAST

▼ Cas-en-Bas to Donkey Beach

Donkey Beach is one of a string of isolated dollops of sand along the rough Atlantic coast, accessible by a scenic coastal foot path from nearby Cas-en-Bas Beach.

P.84 ▶ THE NORTHERN TIP AND THE NORTHEAST COAST

Watersports

One of the most attractive aspects of a trip to St Lucia is the variety of watersports on offer. You can dive beneath the island's sparkling waters; cruise along its breathtaking coast in a chartered yacht; kayak through a winding river; or parasail off the golden shores of Reduit Beach – for starters.

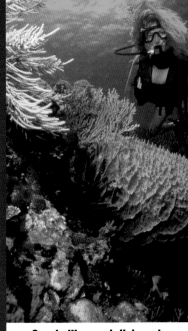

▲ Snorkelling and diving at Anse Chastanet

Dip your snorkelling mask beneath the water's blue-green surface and feast your eyes on an explosion of colour, thanks to the tiny bodies of darting fish and gently waving corals.

P.102 ▶ SOUFRIÈRE AND THE PITONS

▼ Deep-sea fishing

The iridescent dorado fish is among the many kings of the sea you can catch off St Lucia's shores, via a turn on a chartered fishing boat.

P.155 ▶ ESSENTIALS

◀ Sailing from Rodney Bay and Marigot Bay

Rodney and Marigot bays are favoured anchorages among the yachting set; for the boatless, several operators offer sailing trips from both marinas.

P.69 & P.90 ▶ RODNEY BAY AND GROS ISLET & THE WEST COAST

▶ Windsurfing at Anse de Sables

At the southern tip of St Lucia, the heaving Atlantic Ocean is tempered by Pointe Sable and Cap Moule à Chique, but retains enough of its energy to provide windsurfers a fun romp over the waves.

P.121 ▶ THE SOUTH COAST

◀ Parasailing at Reduit Beach

Stop by the waterside concession stand at Reduit Beach to sign up for parasailing, among other activities.

P.69 ▶ RODNEY BAY AND GROS ISLET

▶ Sea kayaking along the southwest coast

Spend the day paddling around the area's limpid turquoise waters; exploring the honey-combed shoreline; or winding your way inland on a coastal river.

P.155 ▶ ESSENTIALS

Plantations

For about a hundred years, beginning in the mid-eighteenth century, St Lucia's European colonizers struggled to establish and maintain sugar and cocoa plantations, relying on slave labour from Africa and later indentured workers from India. Although the land is fertile, the island's mountainous terrain made plantation agriculture difficult, and the profit margin was narrow for most landowners. Some plantations have survived into the twenty-first century by diversifying production; others, long abandoned, have been restored to offer visitors a glimpse into a bygone era.

▲ Fond Doux Estate

Learn about the cocoa-making process (and sample some goods) at this gorgeous, 250-year-old working plantation.

P.108 ▶ SOUFRIÈRE AND THE PITONS

▲ La Sikwi Sugar Mill

One of the few sugar mills on the island built by British settlers, today this estate – which exports flowers and cocoa – is picturesque in its decay.

▼ Balenbouche Estate

Arawak artifacts, the ruins of an eighteenth-century sugar mill and a genteel estate house are on view at this lushly overgrown sugar plantation.

▶ Morne Coubaril Estate

A good walking tour of this 250-acre working estate is conducted by costumed guides, and guided hikes starts at nearby Sulphur Springs and end at the Morne Coubaril hill, on the plantation grounds.

Local markets

Saturday morning is market time on St Lucia, making for a conspicuous hustle and bustle of local shoppers in village squares and market grounds around the island. On other days, you can buy fresh fish right off the boat, or join the daily mêlée of commerce at Castries Central Market.

▲ Castries craft market

A good place to look for a souvenir made in St Lucia – or China.

P.54 ▶ CASTRIES

▲ Fish markets

Fishermen haul in their catch in the early morning and sell it off their boats in communities around the island, including Soufrière in the south and Marisule Beach in the north.

P.60 & P.100 ▶ CASTRIES & SOUFRIÈRE AND THE PITONS

▲ Soufriére's Saturday morning market

Heaps of ripe fruits and vegetables, fresh fish, herbs and spices and the odd hog's head are on offer here.

P.100 ▶ SOUFRIÈRE AND THE PITONS

▼ Castries Central Market

You'll encounter a striking mix of sounds, smells and tastes at the island's largest market.

P.54 ▶ CASTRIES

Gourmet eating

Several of St Lucia's resorts boast spectacularly situated restaurants with sublime gourmet menus and wine lists to match. Their talented chefs draw on fresh local produce and seafood to create dishes that incorporate elements of spicy Creole cooking, as well as Asian, Italian, French and Indian traditions.

▼ Dasheene

West Indian, Asian and Italian dishes are offered in a spectacular setting that takes in views of the Pitons.

P.112 ▶ SOUFRIÈRE AND THE PITONS

▼ Tao

Excellent East/West fusion cuisine, a gorgeous locale overlooking the bay and impeccable service make this one of the island's best dining experiences.

P.89 ▶ THE NORTHERN TIP AND THE NORTHEAST COAST

▲ Mago Estate

This luxurious, candlelit restaurant carved out of the hillside above Soufrière is perfect for those who have romance on the mind.

P.114 ▸ SOUFRIÈRE AND THE PITONS

▼ Great House

This marble-floored mansion is a great spot for dinner or an afternoon tea party.

P.88 ▸ THE NORTHERN TIP AND THE NORTHEAST COAST

▲ Piti Piton and Treehouse Restaurant

Memorable, mouthwatering cuisine is made with fresh local ingredients and served on a cliffside terrace.

P.114 ▸ SOUFRIÈRE AND THE PITONS

▶ Rainforest Hideaway

A cosy and romantic floating champagne bar and restaurant featuring live jazz.

P.98 ▸ THE WEST COAST

Casual bites

You don't need to put on your heels and blow your bank account to enjoy a wonderful meal on St Lucia. Creole cooking is a tasty invention, and the island boasts numerous masters of the traditional repertoire. There are also several casual eateries serving good food in lovely settings, making for a rewarding and inexpensive dining experience.

▲ The Old Plantation Yard

Enjoy stewed meats, fish broths and traditional Creole breakfasts, and maybe hear some impromptu St Lucian folk music.

P.125 ▸ THE SOUTH COAST

▼ Anse La Raye Fish Fry

Sample traditional home-cooked St Lucian dishes at this spirited weekly street party.

P.93 ▸ THE WEST COAST

▲ La Panache

Every Wednesday, the proprietors of this cheerful Gros Islet guesthouse lay on a memorable Creole buffet.

P.79 ▸ RODNEY BAY & GROS ISLET

▲ Spinnakers

This popular beach bar and restaurant is right on the sand at Reduit Beach.

P.81 ▸ RODNEY BAY & GROS ISLET

▲ Café Claude's

One of the best spots for a good meal on the Reduit Beach Drive restaurant strip, offering casual but sophisticated fare on a shady verandah.

P.77 ▸ RODNEY BAY & GROS ISLET

◀ Fox Grove Inn

Expertly prepared meals are served amid panoramic views of the east coast.

P.133 ▸ THE EAST COAST

Nightlife

You can find something to do every night of the week on St Lucia, although most evening entertainment is confined to hotel bars and lounges and unassuming rum shops. Several communities host weekend street parties, with barbeques and fish frys, and each major town has a few hotspots where you can relax with the locals and usually catch some live music.

▲ Pointe Sable Beach Resort

Live it up with the locals at *Pointe Sable Beach Resort*'s Thursday night karaoke.

P.125 ▸ THE SOUTH COAST

▼ Gros Islet's Friday night Jump Up

This well-attended weekly street party encompasses several blocks and lasts well into the night.

P.71 ▸ RODNEY BAY AND GROS ISLET

▶ Rodney Bay

After-dark activity is easy to come by any night of the week along the Reduit Beach Drive restaurant and bar strip.

P.81 ▶ RODNEY BAY AND GROS ISLET

▲ JJ's Paradise Resort

A boardwalk through the mangrove forest leads to a hopping local nightclub.

P.99 ▶ THE WEST COAST

▼ Local rum shops

Every village on the island has at least a couple of bare-bones rum shops where local gents meet to unwind.

P.93 ▶ THE WEST COAST

Scenic retreats

A St Lucian getaway can mean staying anywhere from a luxury resort to a family-oriented hotel to a quaint bed-and-breakfast. But the island's standout accommodation offers dramatic views and secluded locales that are not soon forgotten.

▼ Coco Palm Hotel

This elegant spot, designed with the principles of Feng Shui in mind, is set a bit back from the hubbub of Reduit Beach, but it's still only a few minutes' walk from all the goings-on.

P.74 ▸ RODNEY BAY AND GROS ISLET

▼ Ladera Resort

Stunning views of the sea and the Pitons, beautifully designed rooms and excellent customer service make this exclusive hilltop resort the epitome of luxury.

P.110 ▸ SOUFRIÈRE AND THE PITONS

▶ Ti Kaye Village

For an intimate, romantic experience, it's hard to beat this secluded spot overlooking Anse Cochon.

P.96 ▶ THE WEST COAST

▼ Balenbouche Estate

A wonderfully atmospheric guesthouse and charming cottages are situated on the grounds of an eighteenth-century sugar plantation.

P.123 ▶ THE SOUTH COAST

◀ Anse Chastanet Resort

A marvellous setting, dramatically designed guest suites, exquisite food, a great beach with excellent snorkelling and more – all with the price to match.

P.108 ▶ SOUFRIÈRE AND THE PITONS

St Lucian arts and culture

St Lucia has a rich heritage of literature, theatre, visual arts and music. Island culture is showcased and celebrated in a series of public festivals held throughout the year, but you can always read the work of celebrated local poets; visit intimate galleries; watch artisans in their studios; see well-preserved examples of classic West Indian architecture; and seek out traditional chak chak music or contemporary jazz at several spots around the island.

▲ Pottery and basketry

St Lucia's Amerindian heritage is evident in the pottery and basketry made by island artisans, particularly in the settlement of La Pointe Caribe on the south coast.

P.118 ▸ THE SOUTH COAST

▲ Artwork of Dunstan St Omer

Painter Dunstan St Omer, called the Michelangelo of St Lucia, is best known for his colourful, epic frescos and murals, including those found on the ceiling of the Cathedral of the Immaculate Conception in Castries.

P.54 ▸ CASTRIES

▼ West Indian architecture

Soufrière, established in the mid-eighteenth century, has managed to preserve many of its historic buildings, featuring second-floor balconies and intricate fretwork.

P.100 ▸ SOUFRIÈRE AND THE PITONS

▲ Creole music

Catch some traditional St Lucian folk music at public festivals like International Creole Day.

P.158 ▸ ESSENTIALS

Historical attractions

Beautiful St Lucia has been called "The Helen of the West Indies," fought over in the past by a seemingly constant stream of suitors. The peaceful Arawak people – probably the first inhabitants of the island – were driven out by the Caribs, who were in turn displaced by Europeans, who then turned on each other. Today the island is filled with remnants of St Lucia's violent past, as well as more unassuming attractions that belie a tumultuous history.

▲ Stonefield Estate

On the grounds of this former plantation – now the site of an upscale resort – you can view Arawak petroglyphs dating from 350 AD.

P.111 ▸ SOUFRIÈRE AND THE PITONS

▲ Fort Charlotte

Captured from the French and renamed by the British in 1803, Fort Charlotte, in the hills above Castries, holds Inniskilling Monument, which marks the site of the final bloody battle between the two colonizers.

P.58 ▶ CASTRIES

▼ La Toc Battery

One of St Lucia's best-preserved British military garrisons, this 2.5-acre, nineteenth-century fortification features mounted cannons, dim underground bunkers and more. The grounds also include a small botanical garden and stunning views of Castries harbour.

P.57 ▶ CASTRIES

▲ Pigeon Island

Occupied by a French pirate and later fortified by the British, today you can view everything from military ruins to a cemetery to an informative video in the interpretive centre.

P.70 ▶ RODNEY BAY AND GROS ISLET

Waterfalls and gardens

St Lucia's verdant lushness is showcased in several cool, shady gardens filled with exotic flowering trees and an almost infinite variety of plants that thrive in the tropical climate. There are also numerous natural waterfalls spilling out of the mountains; some feature cool, inviting pools perfect for a hot afternoon, while others are filled with water warmed in the Earth's crust before reaching the surface.

▲ Toraille Falls

Sit in the pool beneath the 15-metre cascade, or hike the upper trail behind the falls.

P.104 ▸ SOUFRIÈRE AND THE PITONS

▲ Mamiku Gardens

Fifteen lush acres bloom with exotic flowers and trees.

P.129 ▸ THE EAST COAST

▼ Sault Falls

One of the prettiest falls on the island, with a large pool below.

P.132 ▸ THE EAST COAST

▲ Anse La Raye Waterfalls

Stop in for a welcome dip after a scenic hike along the riverbank.

P.94 ▸ THE WEST COAST

▶ Warm Mineral Waterfalls

A warm mix of spring water and thermal volcanic emissions streams down into a natural heated pool.

P.108 ▸ SOUFRIÈRE AND THE PITONS

▼ Diamond Botanical Gardens

Warm mineral baths and a waterfall are surrounded by lovingly tended tropical gardens.

P.103 ▸ SOUFRIÈRE AND THE PITONS

Great views

St Lucia is a superbly photogenic island, and everywhere you look you're bound to see beauty. However, if you have just a few shots left on your memory card, save them for the breathtaking panoramas mentioned here. Together, they reveal the island's defining features from their best angles.

▲ From Gros Piton

Views from the rocky summit of Gros Piton take in everything from neighbouring Martinique to the north and St Vincent to the south.

P.106 ▸ SOUFRIÈRE AND THE PITONS

▲ From Pointe Hardy

Take in the sweeping vista down the dramatic, windswept Atlantic coast.

P.83 ▸ THE NORTHERN TIP AND THE NORTHEAST COAST

▼ From Fox Grove Inn

A panoramic view of pretty blue-and-white Praslin Bay, with lush, banana-clad slopes in the foreground, can be had from here.

P.133 ▶ THE EAST COAST

▲ From Cap Moule à Chique

This hilly promontory on St Lucia's southern coast offers a breathtaking gander up the mountainous, forested spine of the island all the way to its northern tip.

P.120 ▶ THE SOUTH COAST

Excursions

If you can rouse yourself out of the hammock or beach lounger, St Lucia offers a myriad of exciting ways to spend the day – more than enough to fill an action-packed holiday. Local tour operators make it easy for visitors, with well-planned day-trips that generally include transportation from your hotel and a range of options that will take you into all parts of the island.

▲ Mountain biking

Adrenaline junkies can bump along more than a dozen kilometres of trails on a lush sugar plantation at Anse Mamin in the south. More sedate country-road tours are offered on the northeast coast.

P.103 ▸ SOUFRIÈRE AND THE PITONS

▲ Horseback rides along the northeast coast

The saddle offers a unique vantage point from which to view the countryside; most rides end up in the surf at Cas-en-Bas beach.

P.84 ▸ THE NORTHERN TIP AND THE NORTHEAST COAST

▲ Helicopter tours

Take in sweeping views of St Lucia's coastline, interior rainforests and more from the
sky.

P.149 ▸ ESSENTIALS

▼ Boat cruises

For a fun day in the sun, hop aboard an
eighteenth-century pirate ship or a sleek
modern catamaran and cruise the west coast,
stopping to take in the sights along the way.

P.148 ▸ ESSENTIALS

Local cuisine

St Lucia offers a variety of taste sensations. The rich soil yields a huge variety of fruits and vegetables, ripened naturally by strong tropical sunlight and picked hours or minutes before they end up on your table. The melding of the various ethnic groups that settled St Lucia has created a national cuisine featuring elements of its diverse cultural origins.

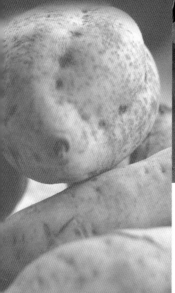

▲ Cocoa tea

This hot local breakfast drink is made with milk, grated cocoa sticks, spices and a little sugar.

P.108 ▸ SOUFRIÈRE AND THE PITONS

▲ Cassava bread

Cassava was originally brought to St Lucia from South America by the Arawaks, and is still cultivated and made into bread today.

P.94 ▸ THE WEST COAST

▶ Creole cooking

A vibrant, mildly spicy melange of traditional African, French and West Indian cooking that incorporates fresh fish and produce grown on St Lucia.

P.152 ▸ ESSENTIALS

▼ Seafood

Buy it right off the boat or have the catch of the day cooked up by one of the island's great chefs.

P.60 & P.100 ▸ CASTRIES & SOUFRIÈRE AND THE PITONS

▲ Ground provisions

Plantains, dasheen and other starchy vegetables were originally grown as food for slaves but are today part of traditional Creole cuisine.

P.153 ▸ ESSENTIALS

▼ Rum

Rum-making continues to be a major contributor to the island's economy. Visit St Lucia Distillers and taste the goods.

P.92 ▸ THE WEST COAST

Flora and fauna

St Lucia offers visitors interested in nature the opportunity to see a huge diversity of flora and fauna, including several species of birds found nowhere else on earth. Even those who don't know a dandelion from an orchid can enjoy the unspoiled beauty of the island's interior and great stretches of coastline.

▲ Ginger lilies

The ginger lily is not native to St Lucia, but its tropical lushness is symbolic of the verdant island.

P.137 ▶ THE CENTRAL INTERIOR

▲ Leatherback turtles

Giant sea turtles come ashore once a year to lay their eggs along the coast, and the long beach at Grand Anse is a favoured nesting spot.

P.86 ▶ THE NORTHERN TIP AND THE NORTHEAST COAST

▼ Fer-de-lance snake and boa constrictors

St Lucia's only poisonous creature, the forest-dwelling fer-de-lance snake, is rarely seen, but you might spot a boa constrictor sunning itself in a tree.

P.137 ▶ THE CENTRAL INTERIOR

▲ Banana plants

While banana production is no longer the backbone of St Lucia's economy, the island is still covered with acres of fertile banana plantations.

P.92 ▶ THE WEST COAST

◀ St Lucian Parrot

The rainbow-coloured St Lucian parrot can only be found on this island.

P.137 ▶ THE CENTRAL INTERIOR

▼ Birds

The island's forests are filled with song birds, including three kinds of hummingbirds, and the Fregate Islands Nature Reserve is named for the seagoing frigate bird that nests here between May and July.

P.132 & P.137 ▶ THE EAST COAST & THE CENTRAL INTERIOR

St Lucian calendar

A predominantly Catholic society, St Lucia marks many of the feast days of the saints – but with a unique flair. The annual calendar also holds several internationally popular events, including Carnival and the St Lucia Jazz Festival, which both offer great performances in spectacular outdoor settings. If you plan to attend either of these two festivals, or even plan to be on the island while they are underway, you should book your accommodation well in advance.

▲ The Feast of St Lucy in December

The island's namesake is honoured with food, dancing and games, and the Christmas season is ushered in with calypso carols and the Festival of Lights.

P.158 ▸ ESSENTIALS

▲ The Feast of St Rose de Lima in August

Members of the antiquated La Rose flower society dress up in stylized eighteenth-century garb and elect a king and queen at their annual celebration.

P.158 ▸ ESSENTIALS

▲ Carnival in July

The island's biggest party features parades, calypso contests and lots of food.

P.158 ▸ ESSENTIALS

▶ Jounen Kwéyòl Entenasyonnal in October

Held in Castries and three villages selected annually, St Lucia's version of International Creole Day features large, open-air celebrations with traditional music, food, sports and dancing.

P.158 ▸ ESSENTIALS

▼ St Lucia Jazz Festival in May

St Lucia's big jazz event draws famous international performers as well as strong local talent.

P.157 ▸ ESSENTIALS

St Lucian pastimes

Many of St Lucia's favourite pastimes have been picked-up from other cultures. Joining in or watching the goings-on is one of the best ways to get to know St Lucian culture and to see locals amid their daily lives.

▼ Playing dominoes

Originally introduced to St Lucia by bored British soldiers, today you can pick up a game – if you know the rules – at any rum shop around the island.

P.93 ▶ THE WEST COAST

▼ Cricket

Catch a match at Beausejour Cricket Ground, near Gros Islet, where St Lucia will host the Cricket World Cup in 2007.

P.70 ▶ RODNEY BAY AND GROS ISLET

▲ Music

Whether taking in live jazz or traditional Creole tunes at a festival or singing along to canned country-and-western in a roadside bar, music occupies a conspicuous place in St Lucians' daily lives.

P.157 ▸ ESSENTIALS

▼ Liming

"Liming" is the Caribbean word for just hanging around. St Lucia has no shortage of places to practise this fine art.

P.79 ▸ RODNEY DAY AND GROS ISLET

Places

Derek

GRANDE ANSE/ DES B
Turtle
Watch

Castries

Home to more than a third of the island's population, Castries feels stuck between a centuries-old lifestyle and a desperate push to modernize. The classic West Indian look of brightly painted wood and intricate gingerbread fretwork has largely been lost due to several major fires that destroyed most of the original colonial-era buildings, although remnants remain, particularly along Brazil Street and around Derek Walcott Square.

The capital city is wrapped around the deep harbour of Port Castries, where hundreds of cruise ships dock to unload visitors for a day of duty-free shopping at the city's malls and in the bustling Castries Central Market. The compact downtown consists of a dozen or so blocks of busy streets, sunbaked concrete shops and dusty bus stands, backed by steep tree-clad hills; the outskirts hold some beaches and resorts, along with a few historical sights. You'll only need a short time to see it all, as it isn't particularly well-endowed with museums, cultural venues or even restaurants, cafés and bars; most visitors are here for business or shopping rather than sightseeing.

Derek Walcott Square

Named after St Lucia's Nobel Prize–winning poet and playwright (see box on p.53), Derek Walcott Square is the focal point of Downtown Castries. In the late eighteenth century, following the French Revolution, it was known as the Place d'Armes, and a guillotine was set up here by Republicans anxious to do away with selected members of the nobility. Later it became Promenade Square, and then Columbus Square (in 1892) – despite the fact that Columbus

▼ DEREK WALCOTT SQUARE

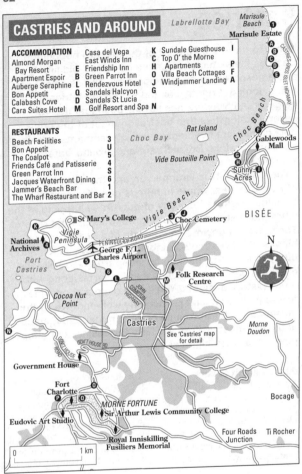

CASTRIES AND AROUND

ACCOMMODATION

Almond Morgan Bay Resort	E	Casa del Vega	K
Apartment Espoir	B	East Winds Inn	C
Auberge Seraphine	L	Friendship Inn	H
Bon Appetit	Q	Green Parrot Inn	O
Calabash Cove	D	Rendezvous Hotel	J
Cara Suites Hotel	M	Sandals Halcyon	G
		Sandals St Lucia Golf Resort and Spa	N
Sundale Guesthouse	I		
Top O' the Morne Apartments	P		
Villa Beach Cottages	F		
Windjammer Landing	A		

RESTAURANTS

Beach Facilities	3
Bon Appetit	U
The Coalpot	5
Friends Café and Patisserie	4
Green Parrot Inn	S
Jacques Waterfront Dining	6
Jammer's Beach Bar	1
The Wharf Restaurant and Bar	2

never set foot on St Lucia – before being given its present name in 1993.

Bordered by bustling Brazil, Micoud, Bourbon and Laborie streets – the oldest and most attractive parts of the capital – this grassy, landscaped oasis in an otherwise congested town serves as a favoured lunchtime spot for local office workers grabbing a quick bite. It is also a pleasant spot for a picnic, with supplies

available at the nearby market or grocery stores. The east side of the square is shaded by an immense saman tree, thought to be more than 400 years old. The small gazebo adjacent to the tree is used for public gatherings and band concerts; it is one of the main venues for the St Lucia Jazz Festival in May (see p.157). A memorial and plaque dedicated to native St Lucians who died during both

Derek Walcott

Poet and playwright **Derek Walcott**, a native St Lucian born in 1930, was educated at St Mary's College in Castries and at the University of the West Indies in Jamaica. His poetry was first published when he was just 18. After moving to New York in the late 1950s, he attended acting school and, in 1959, returned to the Caribbean and established the **Trinidad Theatre Workshop** in Port of Spain. Walcott continued to publish poems and plays throughout the 1960s and his first collection of poetry, *Another Life* (1973), established him as one of the world's most eminent poets. Among his more than 45 major works are the play *Dream on Monkey Mountain* (1970) and the 1990 epic *Omeros*, a broad narrative that mixes Homeric legend with West Indian themes.

Walcott's ethnic origins are British, Dutch and African, and his culture French and British with an American twist, but his sensibility is wholly West Indian. In awarding Walcott the Nobel Prize, the academy commented that "In him, West Indian culture has found its great poet", and called his work "a poetic oeuvre of great luminosity, sustained by a historical vision, the outcome of a multicultural achievement".

world wars occupies the west end of the square, where you'll also find the imposing Victorian redbrick Central Library, built by American philanthropist Andrew Carnegie.

Brazil Street

On the south side of Derek Walcott Square, Brazil Street is the city's crowded and frenetic architectural showcase. By the early twentieth century, Castries'

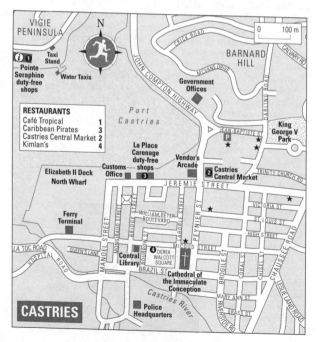

population had burgeoned, and the streets were packed full of warehouses, homes and shacks – most made of wood and piled alongside each other like matches in a box. As it turned out, the resemblance was perhaps a little too close: in May 1927 a large fire swept through the Downtown area, destroying half the city, and in June 1948, another tremendous blaze levelled almost the entire town. Miraculously, several of the structures on Brazil Street facing Derek Walcott Square escaped these fires, and excellent examples of colonial West Indian architecture line the square.

Cathedral of the Immaculate Conception

Corner of Laborie and Micoud sts ✆452-2271. Services Sat 7.30pm, Sun 6am & 7.30am, Children's Mass Sun 10.30am. The cornerstone of the island's Catholic faith is the imposing brick-and-mortar Cathedral of the Immaculate Conception, which seats two thousand communicants. While the site has been occupied by various churches since the early eighteenth century, all of which were destroyed by successive fires and storms, the foundation of the current structure dates to 1894, though today's building was not completed until 1931. The church was granted the status of a cathedral in 1957, and Pope John Paul II visited when he toured the Caribbean in 1986. Unless Mass is in progress, you can look around the ornate interior, bathed in rich red and diffused yellow light from ceiling

portals and busy with detailed carved wood inlay, wooden benches, iron ceiling supports and stately pillars. Note the remarkably colourful ceiling paintings of Catholic saints and apostles, with St Lucie in the centre, and the vivid wall murals, depicting black saints and the work of the Catholic Church on the island, painted before the arrival of Pope John Paul II by island artist **Dunstan St Omer**, who also designed St Lucia's flag.

Castries Central Market

Jeremie St. Mon–Sat 9am–5pm, Sun cruise ship days only. Exuberant, vividly colourful and often loud, the enclosed Central Market is one of the busiest parts of Castries and a must-see for visitors. This rambling, unplanned structure actually houses several markets, all of which are at their most frenetic on Saturday mornings. Inside, rows of **craft booths** accommodate vendors selling baskets, spices, carvings, T-shirts, straw hats and tacky souvenirs. The prices here are about as good as they get, and certainly better than at Pointe Seraphine (see p.64), but they do tend to increase a little if a cruise ship is in town. In the centre of the craft section is a non-functioning cement fountain

▼ CASTRIES CENTRAL MARKET

▲ CASTRIES HARBOUR

resplendent with protruding lion heads painted bright red. The fountain is the most obvious remnant of the original market, built in 1894; you can also still see parts of the old iron structure in the ceiling and walls.

Under an orange roof to the left of the Jeremie Street entrance, the fruit and vegetable market offers a wealth of exotic fresh produce: mangoes, sugar cane, soursop, plantains, earth-encrusted tubers of dasheen and more are piled high on cardboard boxes or makeshift stands of wood. There are also open-air stalls at the back of the market, where, on the north side, you'll find an alleyway of fifteen or so small, steam- and smoke-belching restaurant stalls (see p.65), filling the air with tempting aromas.

Port Castries

Both the French and British colonial powers were drawn to St Lucia by its deep, protected natural harbour surrounded by hills that afforded lookouts to nearby Martinique and to passing ships. In 1651, French settlers built a bastion on the peninsula now called Vigie, on the northern edge of the cove that would become Castries. The settlement grew over the years, and by 1767 the population had shifted south to the banks of the river that flowed into the deep harbour known as Petit Cul de Sac by the French. The settlement was renamed in 1785 in honour of the Marquis de Castries, a minister of the French navy and one of the architects of French military efforts in the Caribbean.

The town of Castries has flourished as a **port** since the seventeenth century, despite successive fires and several disastrous hurricanes – not to mention the minor interruption of the French Revolution, which saw Republicans descend on the island to round up and execute selected members of the French nobility. Castries remained a busy port throughout nineteenth-century British rule, becoming an important **refuelling station** for coal-burning steamships on long ocean voyages, and a convenient stopover for massive cargo and military ships. The port expanded steadily, and new docks and piers were built throughout the twentieth century. In the 1940s, coaling gave way to the export of bananas and, as the market for Caribbean bananas has fallen off dramatically over the past decade, multi-storey cruise ships and tourists have replaced banana boats in Castries harbour.

▲ VIGIE BEACH

Vigie Peninsula

The high rounded hump of the Vigie Peninsula, which frames the northern half of Port Castries and is a short walk, drive or water-taxi ride around the harbour from Downtown, was the original site of the Castries settlement. Today it is home to the George F.L. Charles Airport; nearby Vigie Beach; the Pointe Seraphine duty-free shopping centre; and a few hotels and restaurants.

Sandwiched between the airport runway and the sea, Peninsular Road runs east to west along the length of the peninsula, becoming Nelson Mandela Drive as it climbs the hill. To get on to it, take the John Compton Highway north from Downtown, turn right on the Castries-Gros Islet Highway, left at the end of the airport and left again onto Nelson Mandela Drive. Just before you reach the airstrip, the Choc Cemetery is on the right, typical of those in the Caribbean with its ornately decorated raised white tombs. Forty simple white memorial stones standing sentry around a large white cross designate the War Cemetery section, dedicated to local sailors who were killed in March 1942, when a German submarine skulked into Castries harbour and torpedoed two British ships.

Just west of the cemetery, Peninsular Road flanks the two-kilometre **Vigie Beach**; long and smooth, but with sometimes litter-strewn, brown-grey sand, it's not much to look at – however, the water is usually calm and inviting. A few snack vendors are parked here and there, a handful of benches and picnic tables overlook the water and there's plenty of shade from trees, but for better places to swim and sun yourself, head north to Reduit or south to Marigot.

Once clear of the airport, Peninsular Road winds uphill towards its apex at Vigie Lighthouse. The entire peninsula was once a fortification, and many of the buildings at the top of the hill are restored military quarters (which today house government offices), built from redbrick in the late nineteenth century.

At the western end of the peninsula, **St Lucia's National Archives** (☎452-1654. Mon–Thurs 9am–4pm, Fri 9am–2pm. Free.); are housed in a circa 1890 building; inside, you can browse through hundreds of old photos, lithographs, postcards and maps, which provide a good historical perspective of the island.

Folk Research Centre

Morne Pleasant ☎453-1477. Mon–Fri 8.30am–4.30pm. Donation suggested.
Set high in the hills on the east side of Castries at Morne Pleasant, the Folk Research Centre (or Plas Wichès Foklò, in patois) resides in an old estate house originally owned by the

eminent Deveaux family, one of the first French land-owning families on St Lucia. The small museum consists of a somewhat jumbled but informative display of cultural artefacts, including a reproduction of a traditional ti-kay hut and examples of indigenous musical instruments such as the chak chak (condiment tins taped together and filled with seeds), banjo bwa payé (a small banjo) and tambou (a wooden drum with a goatskin head). Also on display are clay pots and a diorama depicting an ancient St Lucian legend of a witch doctor stepping through a magic door. The small research library upstairs holds one of the island's best collections of books, papers and photographs relating to St Lucian folklore and popular history.

Since it was established in 1973, the centre has spearheaded the movement to preserve and promote the island's heritage as well as St Lucian Creole; it is especially active during Carnival (see p.158), when you can call in for a schedule of plays, musical performances and related events, which take place throughout the island. The centre is also the focal point of International Creole Day, or Jounen Kwéyòl (see p.158), and runs a programme of lectures within local schools in addition to staging performances by the in-house Popular Theatre group (or Teyat Pep La).

To get to the centre, turn off the Castries–Gros Islet Highway along L'Anse Road, which heads inland just south of the airport, then turn off again at the sign for Morne Pleasant.

La Toc Battery

⌖ 452-7921 or 452-6039. Daily 9am–3pm by appointment only.

EC$13.25. From Downtown Castries, La Toc Road leads west along the south side of the harbour and, about a mile or so on, to La Toc Battery, one of St Lucia's best-preserved British military bastions. This 2.5-acre, nineteenth-century cement fortification features mounted cannons and dim underground bunkers, tunnels and cartridge storage rooms; one of the bunkers holds a large exhibit of antique bottles. If military history doesn't interest you, the superb views down to the southern entrance to Castries harbour almost certainly will, plus there's a small botanical garden where guides conduct tours at no extra cost.

Morne Fortune

Comprising a series of heavily treed hills that overlook the city centre on its southern edge, the attractive suburb of Morne Fortune (also known as "The Morne" and meaning "Good Luck Hill" in French) provides striking views of the city, the Vigie Peninsula, the north coast (on a clear day you can see Martinique) and to the south as well, with glimpses of the conical Pitons to Soufrière. The main lure of the Morne Fortune hills, however, are the eighteenth- and nineteenth-century military installations of Fort Charlotte and Government House, the historic residence of St Lucia's Governor General.

Government House

Government House Rd, Morne Fortune ⌖ 452-2481, ⊛ www
.stluciagovernmenthouse.com.
Tues & Thurs 10am–noon and 2pm–4pm by appointment only.
Unsurprisingly, the focal point of Government House Road, just south of Downtown

▲ GOVERNMENT HOUSE

Castries, is Government House, an imposing, white Victorian two-storey structure dating from 1895 that serves as the official residence of the Governor General. The building houses the small Le Pavillon Royal Museum, where you can see a collection of artefacts and documents relating to the history of the house, photographs and documents pertaining to past prime ministers and significant modern St Lucian artefacts. A viewing platform set just below the building affords wonderful views of Castries below.

Fort Charlotte

A few winds and turns beyond Government House, Morne Road takes you to the top of the 260-metre Morne Fortune itself. The hills were first fortified by the French in 1768, then recaptured and named Fort Charlotte by the British in 1803. The **Inniskilling Monument** honours the Royal Inniskilling Fusiliers, who fought for many days on the steep slopes to take the position from the French in 1796. Several of the existing military encampments, cemeteries, barracks and batteries have

long been slated to be restored and opened to the public; however, the process is incomplete and many are still in a state of disrepair. Among those that have received some attention is the Apostles' Battery, just off the road south of Government House. Built from 1888 to 1890, it features four mounted ten-inch guns, but the expansive views of the sea from here are probably more eye-catching than the ruin itself. Back on the road and a few hundred metres to the east is Provost's Redoubt, another gun battery, built in 1782, also with gorgeous views to the northwest coast.

The best-preserved remnants of the fort now house offices of the Agricultural Department, the Caribbean Environmental Health Institute and the Organization of Eastern Caribbean States, as well as the **Sir Arthur Lewis Community College**, named after the St Lucian Nobel Prize-winner (see box, opposite), who is buried in a private plot on the grounds. The college comprises several larger, nineteenth-century yellow-brick structures with gleaming white columns, all of military origin, which include the Combermere Barracks, a series of three buildings named

▲ VIEW FROM INNISKILLING MONUMENT

Sir Arthur Lewis

The economist **Sir Arthur Lewis** was born on Antigua in 1915, but emigrated to St Lucia with his family at the age of 3. After completing his secondary education at 14, he won a scholarship to study in England. Of his childhood aspirations, Lewis said, "I wanted to be an engineer, but neither the government nor the sugar plantations would hire a black engineer." So, instead, he studied commerce and accounting at the London School of Economics and earned a PhD in Industrial Economics in 1940.

Lewis taught at the Universities of London and Manchester in England, and in 1959 returned home to the Caribbean to become Vice-Chancellor of the University of the West Indies. In 1963 he moved to Princeton University, where he was a professor until his death at age 76 in 1991.

Lewis was awarded the Nobel Prize in 1978 for his seminal work on economic growth in developing countries, first advanced in an article he wrote in 1954. He spent his career refining this theory and seeking solutions to global poverty, including personal involvement in the establishment of the Caribbean Development Bank in the 1970s. He was knighted for extraordinary service to the realm in 1979.

after Lord Combermere, the commander of British forces in St Lucia between 1817 and 1820. You're free to amble about and visit the buildings and Inniskilling monument, which is on the south side of the college complex behind the Combermere Barracks.

Eudovic Art Studio

Morne Fortune ☏ 452-2747, Mon–Fri 8:30am–4:30pm; Sat & Sun until 3pm. At Eudovic Art Studio, you can watch local wood carvers create some extraordinary works under the watchful eye of master artisan Vincent Joseph Eudovic. One of the island's most renowned carvers, Eudovic studied in Africa and works in mahogany, teak and cedar to produce abstract pieces. He also uses the local wood laurier canelle, found as stumps and buried roots in the rainforests.

Choc Bay

Five minutes out of town and past the peninsula, the highway runs parallel to the two-kilometre sweep of Choc Bay, a broad swath of golden sand backed by coconut palms and flowering trees. The bay is fringed to the north by Labrellotte Point, a compact, sheltered inlet containing a couple of luxury resorts, and to the south by Vide Bouteille Point, a small promontory that separates Choc and Vigie bays and was the site of St Lucia's first fort, built in 1660 by the French (there's nothing left of it today). From the highway, you'll catch tempting glimpses of the hidden coves and honey-coloured sand beaches that pepper Choc

▲ SIR ARTHUR LEWIS COMMUNITY COLLEGE

Bay, some lined by hotels. The beaches are accessible via several turnoffs, but one of the best places to spend a day is the stretch adjacent to The Wharf (see p.66), a lively beach bar.

Marisule Beach

Continuing northward on the Castries–Gros Islet Highway, the turn-off to rocky Marisule Beach is on the left at the traffic light opposite the turn-off to Grand Rivière. On Monday, Wednesday and Friday mornings you can buy fresh fish here right off the boat when the fishermen come back from their early morning run around 9–10am; listen for the sound of the conch shell horn that signals their return.

Labrellotte Bay

A few hundred metres north of Marisule Beach, a small sign on the left (just past Glace Motors, which is on the right) marks the turn-off to the *East Winds Inn* on Labrellotte Bay, a sheltered cove surrounded by steep hillsides dotted with vacation villas and permanent residences. There is a small patch of public beach here connecting the swath of sand in front of the hotel to the longer strand fronting the larger *Windjammer Landing* resort, where there is a pleasant beach bar and restaurant. The road is steep and

rough in places, but passable in a car; alternatively, the beach is a fifteen-minute walk in from the main road, where buses pass frequently.

Accommodation

Almond Morgan Bay Resort

Choc Bay ☎1-800/4-ALMOND (in North America), ⊛www.almondresorts .com. This all-inclusive beach resort is set on 22 seaside acres three miles north of Castries. The grounds include tennis courts, four pools and pathways that wend through gardens, and guests may enjoy activities such as sailing, kayaking, windsurfing and more. Four restaurants seve breakfast, lunch and dinner daily. From $500.

Apartment Espoir

Labrellotte Bay ☎452-8134, ⊛www .apartmentespoir.com. Perched in lush gardens on the hillside overlooking Labrellotte Bay, the *Espoir's* cosy studio and one- and two-bedroom apartments afford spectacular sunset views from private balconies. Rooms at this peaceful spot are simply furnished but very clean, with fully equipped kitchens, TV, a/c and ceiling fans. A five-minute walk brings you to a small public beach or the more enticing strip of sand and adjacent beach bar at *Windjammer Landing.* The genial

▼ ALMOND MORGAN BAY RESORT

owner offers great tours around the island. Studios $60, one-bedroom apartments $75.

Auberge Seraphine

Vieille Bay, Pointe Seraphine ☏456-3000 or 453-2073, ⑩www .aubergeseraphine.com. On a small green inlet on the west side of Pointe Seraphine, this spot is favoured by business travellers for its easy access to Downtown Castries. Each of the 22 spacious and modern upscale rooms has a porch, a/c, cable TV and hair dryer. A patio with a pool and sun deck is above the restaurant. $110.

Bon Appetit

Red Tape Ln, off Morne Rd, Morne Fortune ☏452-2757. The bonus feature of this four-room guest-house in the hills is its small but highly regarded French/West Indian restaurant (see p.64). The rooms are basic, clean and secure, each with private bath, TV and fan; rates include breakfast. $45.

Cara Suites Hotel

La Pansee Rd, east side of Castries ☏452-4767, ⑩www.carahotels.com. High on a hill less than a kilometre from the city centre, this modern business-oriented hotel has 54 pleasant rooms with a/c, cable TV and balconies, as well as a pool and decent restaurant. Functional rather than romantic, it's clean and well-equipped. $100.

Casa Del Vega

Clark Ave, Vigie Peninsula ☏459-0780/720-4001, ⑩www .casadelvega.net. Set high above the city on the tip of the peninsula, this place – with comfortable double rooms and two- and three-bedroom suites – is a bit isolated. But it's a decent budget option if you're planning to rent a car anyway. Doubles $35, suites $80.

East Winds Inn

Labrellotte Bay ☏452-8212, ⑩www.eastwinds.com. This small, low-key, all-inclusive resort is nestled seaside beneath the steep slopes surrounding Labrellotte Bay. The dollhouse-like mint-green-and-white trimmed cottages and a couple of small blocks of rooms are scattered over an expanse of lawn dotted with fruit trees. The rooms are spacious and well appointed, with plunge showers and mini-fridges; the beach is private; the pool is sizeable; and the restaurant is good. Doubles $275, mini-suites $380.

Friendship Inn

Castries-Gros Islet Hwy, Sunny Acres ☏452-4201. Each room in this pleasant, no-frills roadside accommodation is equipped with a/c, cable TV, a telephone and a kitchenette. There's a swimming pool, plus Choc Beach is within walking distance. $65.

Green Parrot Inn

Morne Fortune ⓣ452-3399 or 452-3167. Slightly tatty and infused with the air of a former hot-spot, this 55-room inn south of Castries offers a chance to wallow in the coolish breezes drifting up the hills. The restaurant's West Indian cuisine is a real draw, as is its alfresco seating with views of Castries below. There's also a pool, and the hotel provides complimentary transport to local beaches. $80.

Rendezvous Hotel

Vigie Beach ⓣ457-7900, ⓦwww.theromanticholiday.com. Billing itself as "the escape for romantics", this sprawling seven-acre, couples-only, all-inclusive on the beach has tons of watersports and amenities, including hot tubs, two pools, tennis, fitness rooms, scuba diving, golf and nightly entertainment as well as a couple of restaurants and bars. The vast rooms are luxurious and designed with honeymooners in mind, though the concept may prove too formulaic for some. From $500.

Sandals Halcyon and Sandals Regency St Lucia Golf Resort and Spa

Halcyon: Choc Bay ⓣ453-0222 or 1-800/726-3247 (US). Regency St Lucia: La Toc Bay ⓣ452-3081 or 1-800/726-3247 (US), ⓦwww.sandals.com. The beaches are wide and the water is calm at these two Sandals resorts. The chain's all-inclusive formula for success – generic island fun – is no different here than in Jamaica, where Sandals originated and gained its reputation for fine food, extensive sports facilities, luxury rooms and a lovey-dovey atmosphere. *Sandals Regency St Lucia* is the larger of the two, with a nine-hole golf course and spa, but guests at either resort can access the beaches, nine restaurants and amenities of both via an hourly shuttle; additionally, access is available to the facilities at *Sandals Grande Resort*, north of Rodney Bay (see p.67). No kids and no singles allowed. *Halcyon* from $560; *Regency St Lucia* from $650.

Sundale Guesthouse

Sunny Acres ⓣ452-4120, ⓔpeterkingshott@hotmail.com. The Kingshotts' small guesthouse on a side road near the Gablewoods Mall is scrupulously clean, inexpensive and within walking distance of Choc Bay's beaches and the Gablewoods Mall. Rooms have verandahs, fans and private baths, and the three one-bedroom apartments (with kitchens and TV) can sleep four at a push. There's a communal lounge with a TV and VCR, and a kitchen for guests' use. No credit cards. Doubles $40; one-bedroom apartments. $50.

Top O' the Morne Apartments

Morne Fortune ⓣ452-3603, ⓦwww.topothemorne.com. Once used to house British officers, today this 150-year-old building comprises nine apartments available on a nightly or long-term basis. While the bricks are showing their age, the spacious, high-ceilinged rooms are tastefully decorated with tile floors and dark wood furniture accented with colourful rugs and linens. Offers spectacular harbour views, large verandahs, a pool and high-speed Internet access. Though a bit out of the way, this is a nice, quiet choice if you have a car. Studio $90, one-bedroom apartment $130. Room, car and all taxes for a week $1190. Discounts apply for longer-term stays.

Villa Beach Cottages

Choc Bay ☎450-2884, ⓦwww .villabeachcottages.com. A tidy clutch of whitewashed wooden cottages, villas and villa suites – all with full kitchens, a/c, TV, Internet access, and deep verandahs with hammocks – sit on a narrow strip of land between the road and the beach. There is also a small restaurant and bar. Cottages $120, villas $205, villa suites $180.

Windjammer Landing

Labrellotte Bay ☎456-9000, 1-800/345-0356 (Canada and the US), 44(0) 870/160-9645 (Europe), 1-800/858-4618 (US), ⓦwww .eliteislandresorts.com. Sprawling over 55 hillside acres on and above Labrellotte Bay, this is the nicest resort in the Castries area. Accommodation includes well-appointed rooms and gorgeous whitewashed villas – some with private pools, personal chefs, and lovely water views. Getting around is a bit of a hassle given the steep incline of the property, but minivans shuttle you along the winding lanes from your room to the five resort restaurants (three waterside), four pools and fine sandy beach, where watersports are on offer. Double $250; one-bedroom villa $400.

Shops

Vendor's Arcade

Across from the Central Market on Peynier Street, and easily identifiable by the rust-coloured roof, the Vendor's Arcade is a set of craft stalls selling rather tacky souvenirs at relatively high prices.

La Place Carenage

Jeremie St. Mon–Fri 9am–4pm, Sat 9am–1pm, and, if cruise ships are visiting, some shops open Sun 9am

▲ WINDJAMMER LANDING

to 4pm. The duty-free Place Carenage is about a five-minute walk west from the Central Market. La Carenage, or "the place for careening" (scraping the barnacles off and recaulking the bottom of boats), was the first name of the settlement now known as Castries. The centre has several craft and vegetable stalls, art galleries and boutiques, and you'll find some good deals here, without the trouble of travelling over the water to the large mall at Pointe Seraphine (see below). Remember to bring both your passport and your airline ticket if you plan to take advantage of the duty-free prices though. There's a tourist information booth here, as well as a booking office for Heritage Tours (see p.149). Upstairs, on the third floor, the Animation Centre offers a twenty-minute audio-visual overview of St Lucian history.

Pointe Seraphine

Vigie Peninsula. Mon–Fri 9am–5pm, Sat 9am–2pm. Outside the usual Caribbean tourist paraphernalia and comestibles, Castries is not a shopper's paradise; yet at the north end of the inner harbour you'll find the duty-free Pointe Seraphine, built in the early 1990s. Two adjacent cruise ship berths deliver disembarking tourists directly to the stores, while the taxi stand (☎452-1733) and the water taxi to Downtown Castries are there to cater to the day-trippers. The twenty-plus shops include international chain stores, as well as local retailers dealing in leather goods, cigars, music, souvenirs and art. You'll also find a branch of the National Commercial Bank and the Sunshine Bookshop here – the latter stocks a selection of British and US newspapers, as well as local papers. There is also a small café and a bar, good for a bite while shopping but not worth a special trip.

Restaurants

Beach Facilities

Vigie Beach ☎452-5494. Mon–Sat 10am–2am. On the beach at the east end of the airport runway, a collection of shacks offers hearty local food – mutton stew, fried fish, curried chicken etc. Prices range from EC$5 to EC$10 for a filling lunch or dinner. No credit cards.

Bon Appetit

Red Tape Ln, off Morne Rd, Morne Fortune ☎452-2757. Mon–Fri 11am–2pm & 6.30–9.30pm, Sat & Sun 6.30–9.30pm. You'll feel much like you're dining in a private home at this small guesthouse in the Castries hills, open by reservation only. The brief menu (entrees range from EC$25–55) includes green-skinned pumpkin soup and crab thermadore – smallish servings tastefully arranged and embellished with heavy sauces. Hand-painted pastels on the walls are as soothing as the views of the harbour below.

Café Tropical

Pointe Seraphine ☎452-7411. This cheerful little nook serves weary duty-free shoppers inexpensive lunches of baked lamb, fish creole, fish and chips and burgers, as well as cool drinks and tropical cocktails.

Caribbean Pirates

La Place Carenage ☎452-2543. Mon–Thurs 8am–7pm, Fri & Sat 8am–11pm, Sun cruise ship days only. On the

▲ GREEN PARROT INN

Port Castries waterfront, this spot is popular with locals and cruise ship crowds alike. The menu, which changes weekly, features nouvelle Creole cuisine. Seafood is the speciality – if you're feeling adventurous, try the curried turtle. Main dishes range in price from EC$15 to EC$40.

Castries Central Market

Jeremie St, Castries ☎ 453-1019. Daily 6am–evening. Vendors, shoppers and local business people flock to eat breakfast or lunch at the dozen or so restaurant stalls in the small, crowded alleyway behind the market. Taken at unadorned plastic tables, the servings of seafood, rotis, rice and beans or meat and dumplings are hearty and delicious. Most stalls don't accept credit cards.

The Coalpot Restaurant

Vigie Marina ☎ 452-5566, ☎ www .coalpotrestaurant.com. Mon–Fri lunch & dinner, Sat dinner only. Dinner reservations are essential at the *Coalpot*, which is one of the island's busiest and best restaurants. The expensive cuisine (entrees range from EC$30 to EC$70) is a fusion of French and St Lucian cultures,

with choices including lobster bisque flavoured with cognac and St Lucian callaloo soup to start. Main courses are design-your-own: pair your choice of fresh local seafood or meat with your favourite sauce. Located directly on the water's edge, with a dark interior embellished with local artwork, this is a perfect place for a special night out.

Friends Café and Patisserie

Casa St Lucia, Vigie Peninsula ☎ 458-1335. 7am–7pm Mon–Thurs and Sat; 7am until late Fridays. This stylish, inexpensive little French-style café is situated at the top of the hill in the old military barracks. Coffee and a muffin runs about EC$10; sandwiches and the daily special range from EC$20 to EC$25.

Green Parrot Inn

Morne Fortune ☎ 452-3399 or 452-3167. Daily 7am–late. Irascible chef Harry Edwards trained at the illustrious Claridge's hotel in London, and now he presides over Wednesday and Saturday night floorshows and cooks up Creole, West Indian and international food with flair. The seafood here is great, and there are views down onto Castries

Harbour. Ladies wearing flowers in their hair accompanied by well-dressed gents eat for free on Mondays; otherwise the prix fixe (call for days) is EC$90. The restaurant will pay round-trip taxi fares for groups of four or more, or the one-way fare for parties of two.

Jacques Waterfront Dining

Vigie Marina ☎ 458-1900, ✿ www .froggiejacques.com. Mon–Sat lunch & dinner. Though the name has been changed from the less sophisticated-sounding Froggie Jacques, this place remains a warm and personal waterside bar and restaurant that's big on excellent food and small on overdressed pomp. The emphasis here is on hearty dishes and home-smoked fish, but vegetarians dishes are available and special requests are welcome. Prices are moderate to expensive.

Jammer's Beach Bar

In *Windjammer Landing Resort*, Labrellotte Bay ☎ 456-9000. Daily. At this busy but relaxed beach bar and restaurant, seating is available on multi-level wood decks shaded by palm trees strung with twinkling white lights. The moderately priced menu (entrees range from EC$20 to EC$60) includes sandwiches, salads, salmon quiche, tasty and filling vegetable and seafood rotis, burgers and baked chicken, with coconut and mango cheesecake or banana fritters for dessert.

Kimlan's

22 Micoud St, Derek Walcott Square ☎ 452-1136. Mon–Sat 7am–11pm. Situated above a shop, this popular no-frills lunch counter offers seating on a shaded balcony overlooking the town square. The menu includes Creole dishes, rotis, burgers, fries and ice cream, and lunch is unlikely to cost you more than EC$10–15.

The Wharf Restaurant and Bar

Castries–Gros Islet Hwy, Choc Bay ☎ 450-4844. Daily 9am–6pm. This big, draughty joint serves decent American and Caribbean dishes at moderate prices (EC$20–30 for lunch), but the beach is the main draw. Seaside dining is available at picnic tables on a shaded flagstone terrace; and there are also lounge chairs and a beach volleyball net, making it a popular spot for visitors without hotel beach facilities (especially cruiseship passengers).

Rodney Bay and Gros Islet

The sweeping horseshoe of Rodney Bay is where most of the island's visitor facilities are concentrated. The site of an American army base during WWII, the land at the southern end of the bay has been transformed into Rodney Bay Village, a compact resort area sandwiched between the pretty and popular Reduit Beach and Rodney Bay Marina.

Just to the north and across the channel from Rodney Bay, Gros Islet (GROZ-i-lay) is a small, sun-baked fishing village of rickety, rust-roofed wooden cottages and narrow streets lined with fruit and vegetable vendors. Artefacts that seem to be evidence of Carib and Arawak settlement dating back 1500 years have been found both around Gros Islet and in nearby Pigeon Island National Historic Park, a picturesque spot offering pleasant beaches, stunning views, scenic walking paths, ruins of eighteenth-century British fortifications and a couple of simple eateries.

Rodney Bay Village

Occupying a flat patch of land between the beach and the marina, Rodney Bay Village comprises a few sandy lanes lined with hotels, restaurants, vacation condos, gift stores and a shopping plaza, as well as some

Admiral George Rodney

Admiral George Brydges Rodney (1718–92) looms large in the history of the West Indies, particularly in the bloody Anglo-French conflict over possession of key islands. Rodney entered the British navy at the age of 14 and distinguished himself in his late 20s by leading forces in British naval victories in Martinique.

By 1782, Rodney had established part of his naval force at the Gros Islet harbour, today's Rodney Bay. From military observation points at Pigeon Island he was able to scrutinize French activity off the coast of northern Martinique. In April of that year the French fleet, under **Admiral François de Grasse**, sailed from Martinique, intending to join forces with its Spanish allies at Cap François, Haiti, and then head for Jamaica to attack Fort Charles, one of the largest British strongholds in the West Indies. Rodney countered by sailing his fleet to the Dominica Passage, between Guadeloupe and Dominica, where he cut off and engaged de Grasse's force. A fierce three-day battle ensued, known as the **Battle of the Saints** after the Guadeloupean Iles des Saintes archipelago. The British were victorious – de Grasse and seven French vessels were captured, effectively breaking the back of the French effort in the Caribbean, and Rodney earned the title of baron, bestowed on him by King George III of England.

residential streets in the low hills surrounding the village centre and the bay. Most of the hotels and other tourism infrastructure has sprung up within the last twenty years.

At the beginning of the twentieth century, Gros Islet, as all of this area (Rodney Bay,

Gros Islet Village and Pigeon Island) was once known, was little more than a bucolic fishing village bordered by a great marsh. During World War II, however, Allied forces constructed naval airfields at Gros Islet (and at Vieux Fort) for the defence of the Panama

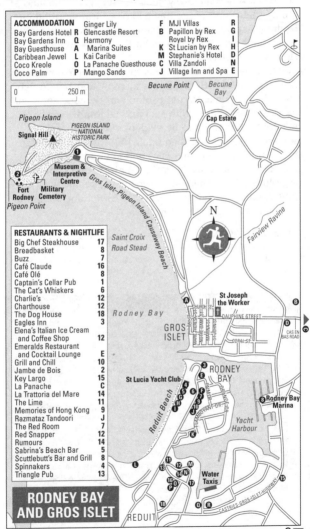

ACCOMMODATION

Bay Gardens Hotel	R	Ginger Lily	F
Bay Gardens Inn	Q	Glencastle Resort	B
Bay Guesthouse	A	Harmony	
Caribbean Jewel	L	Marina Suites	
Coco Kreole	O	Kai Caribe	
Coco Palm	P	La Panache Guesthouse	C
		Mango Sands	J
MJI Villas	R
Papillon by Rex	G
Royal by Rex	I
St Lucian by Rex	H
Stephanie's Hotel	D
Villa Zandoli	N
Village Inn and Spa	E

RESTAURANTS & NIGHTLIFE

Big Chef Steakhouse	17
Breadbasket	8
Buzz	7
Café Claude	16
Café Olé	8
Captain's Cellar Pub	1
The Cat's Whiskers	6
Charlie's	12
Charthouse	12
The Dog House	18
Eagles Inn	3
Elena's Italian Ice Cream and Coffee Shop	12
Emeralds Restaurant and Cocktail Lounge	E
Grill and Chill	10
Jambe de Bois	2
Key Largo	15
La Panache	C
La Trattoria del Mare	14
The Lime	11
Memories of Hong Kong	9
Razmataz Tandoori	J
The Red Room	7
Red Snapper	12
Rumours	14
Sabrina's Beach Bar	5
Scuttlebutt's Bar and Grill	8
Spinnakers	4
Triangle Pub	13

RODNEY BAY AND GROS ISLET

▲ RODNEY BAY HARBOUR

finest in the Caribbean, and, additionally, the Rodney Bay Marina complex offers a few pleasant waterside restaurants as well as banks and gift shops.

Canal and the interests of the United States against the German U-boats and other vessels of war that skulked in the area. Today you can see remnants of concrete loading ramps built by the navy on the raggedy end of the beach at the far end of Reduit Beach Drive.

Rodney Bay Harbour
In 1970, the government dredged the large mangrove swamp south of the village of Gros Islet and let it fill with water to create an inner harbour. The sand and sludge removed from the swamp was used to construct the Pigeon Island causeway (see p.70). The anchorage is considered by many boaters to be among the

Reduit Beach
Vacationers congregate on the hotel and restaurant strip along Reduit (REH-doo-ee) Beach Drive, on the southwest side of Rodney Bay Village. Here they can soak up the sun at one of the dozen or more resorts' pools or sip a cocktail at one of several beachside or sidewalk bars and cafés. The strip fronts the inviting and easily accessible Reduit Beach, the most popular beach on the island for its wide band of golden sand, usually gentle surf, pleasing views of Pigeon Island to the north and the coastal hills to the south and array of watersports. The beach is often packed with well-oiled bodies in high season, and lined almost its entire length (about

▼ REDUIT BEACH

Environmental concerns

The swamp that was dredged to create Rodney Bay Harbour and the Pigeon Island causeway was once a prime breeding and feeding area for hundreds of species of migrating birds and marine life, such as cattle egrets, herons, the St Lucia black finch and oriole as well as prawns, spiny lobster and conch, most of which have now moved elsewhere. The jury remains out regarding deeper **environmental concerns** – the natural filtration systems provided by the swamp are gone, and ocean currents that flowed around Pigeon Island have been interrupted by the causeway. However, tourism development has flourished around Rodney Bay as a result, contributing substantially to the island's economy.

1.6km long) with large-scale but low-lying pastel hotel blocks. The hotels provide chairs and umbrellas for their guests, and many will rent them to visitors staying elsewhere for about EC$26/day.

St Joseph the Worker Roman Catholic Church

Church St, Gros Islet. Though there is little to distinguish Gros Islet in terms of architectural merit, one building worth a look is the imposing St Joseph the Worker Roman Catholic Church on Church Street, a block north of Dauphine Street, the main drag. It's an ornate structure with a cement facade, built in 1926 on the site of a church destroyed by a 1906 earthquake.

Gros Islet–Pigeon Island Causeway Beach

Dotted with fishing boats, drying nets and small vendor huts (as well as some unappealing detritus), the thin public beach along Bay Street is generally quiet and little used. While the water is not very inviting immediately in front of the town, if you walk a few hundred metres further north along the shore you'll find yourself on a lovely, long sweep of white sand that stretches about a kilometre to Pigeon Island, with some shade trees and picnic tables along the way.

Beausejour Cricket Ground

Call the St Lucia Tourist Board for ticket information ☏452-4094. St Lucia will be one of eight hosts of the 2007 Cricket World Cup, with four teams playing matches at the Beausejour Cricket Ground in Gros Islet, signposted off the main Castries-Gros Islet highway. The stadium at Beausejour, set on 22 verdant acres, seats 15,000 spectators.

Pigeon Island National Historic Park

Daily 9am–5pm. EC$10; EC$30 for a 10-day pass; children under 12 EC$1. On February 23, 1979, the day St Lucia gained its independence, Britain's Princess

▲ JUMP UP IN GROS ISLET

Friday Night Jump Up

Generally, there's little of interest for visitors in Gros Islet, but come Friday night, Lucians and guests alike pour in for the **Jump Up** street party, when everyone lets loose. Much of the town is blocked off, and armies of snack vendors peddling barbecue, fried fish, hot cakes and cold beer arrive to feed the masses. Street corners are festooned with speakers, and the canned music is loud. Things get going around 10pm and last until the small hours of the morning. While it's generally a good-natured affair, women should be prepared for unwanted attention and shouldn't attend alone. You're also best off leaving your valuables at home and being extra cautious if walking back to your guesthouse late at night.

Alexandra opened Pigeon Island National Historic Park to the public. Today, this handsome promontory jutting into the ocean just north of Gros Islet is one of St Lucia's most popular relaxation spots – a historic site, concert venue and good place for a hike and a picnic all at once.

In the 1970s, the park was designated a national landmark and some of its buildings have been partially restored. Other sites have been excavated and are now carefully preserved ruins, which visitors can explore at their leisure.

Inside the park boundaries are two small but appealing beaches equipped with toilets and shower facilities. Both beaches are shallow and sheltered by rock jetties that provide calm water, and there are plenty of shady spots under the trees. Pigeon Island's beaches are particularly popular on weekends, when cruise ship passengers ferried in from

Castries add to the usual crowd of locals enjoying a day out.

To get to Pigeon Island, turn west from the Castries–Gros Islet Highway along the causeway, at the exit signposted for the complex.

Pigeon Island Museum and Interpretive Centre

Pigeon Island National Historic Park. After collecting a free map at the entrance, stop by the Pigeon Island Museum and Interpretive Centre on your right, just past the crumbling ruins of an old officers' kitchen. A mini-museum of the island's past, the one-room centre has displays of Amerindian axes, clay bowls, flint and shell tools and antique colonial furniture; a twenty-minute video describing the history of St Lucia in a nutshell is presented at the press of a button.

The centre's gift shop sells history pamphlets and books, souvenirs and locally produced rum. Just below the centre is

Travelling by water

On the waterfront south of the island's fortifications there's a small dock where you can catch the rather expensive tourist **ferries** (EC$25 one-way) to Rodney Bay Marina. It is also possible to take a **water taxi** from Rodney Bay to Pigeon Island (EC$26 round trip; ticket booth on Reduit Beach Drive ⊕452-0087). As taxis and buses will transport you for a fraction of the cost, the ferry is more a fun ride than a necessity.

François Leclerc

One of Pigeon Island's more colourful past inhabitants, **François Leclerc** was a French sea captain turned freebooter nicknamed Jambe de Bois ("wooden leg") for his suitably piratical appendage. Leclerc arrived in the Caribbean sometime around 1550 and used Pigeon Island as a strategic hideout and base for five years. He is believed to have pulled off some sort of truce with the habitually aggressive Caribs, and is known to have captured at least four cargo ships in his time; survivors of these sea battles were either killed or invited to join his buccaneer crew. Leclerc often sank the barren hulks of the ships he stripped for supplies, and legend has it that he secreted treasure somewhere along the northern shore of the island, near Pigeon Point. He moved on sometime after 1554, but no records of his fate exist.

the wonderfully cavernous *Captain's Cellar Pub* (see p.77), a bar housed in the old barracks where you can head for an ice-cold pint of Piton after tackling the island's hills.

Fort Rodney

Pigeon Island National Historic Park. Past the Interpretive Centre, the south side of the park is dotted with the remains of the military barracks and encampments built by the British, including gun batteries, a powder magazine, a lime kiln and what's left of Fort Rodney. Some structures are more intact than others, such as the thick-walled powder magazine to the left of the entrance and the old cooperage near the beach on the south side of the island, which now

houses toilet facilities. You can explore the ruins via the marked walking trails that traverse most of the island, but some of the decaying structures have signs warning visitors off. Every May, impromptu stages are set up in the open spaces among the ruins to host St Lucia Jazz Festival concerts (see p.157); folk performances, local comedy shows featuring Caribbean storytellers, Christmas concerts and monthly music concerts are also held here.

Military cemetery

Pigeon Island National Historic Park. Along the southern shore of Pigeon Island and reachable via one of its hiking trails is a military cemetery, laid out at one of the island's few pieces

The history of Pigeon Island

In 1778, Pigeon Island was fortified by the newly arrived British colonists, and it was from here that Admiral Rodney (see box on p.67) launched the attack against the French that effectively ended their domination of the Caribbean. When African slaves were given their freedom by French Republicans following the French Revolution, imminent British repossession of the island and fear of re-enslavement spurred them into action: tagged as the "**Brigands**", the Africans banded together to create a minor rebellion of their own, razing plantations and even taking brief possession of the heavily fortified Pigeon Island before signing a peace treaty in 1798. Since then the cay served variously as a camp for indentured East Indian labourers and a quarantine station for patients afflicted with the contagious tropical disease known as yaws, and had a brief incarnation as a whaling station between 1909 and 1925.

of flat land. Shaded by tall trees, the weatherbeaten grey and white monuments date back to the late eighteenth century, and commemorate British soldiers and sailors who died defending St Lucia.

Signal Hill

Pigeon Island National Historic Park. Several prominent hillocks dominate Pigeon Island north of the military buildings, with 110-metre Signal Hill being the highest. A marked trail leads right to its base, and from here, it should take about fifteen minutes to reach the peak. It's easy to understand why Signal Hill was designated Pigeon Island's main lookout post: it affords panoramic vistas south to Gros Islet and the outskirts of Castries, and north over the expanse of the St Lucia Channel to the island of Martinique.

Accommodation

Bay Gardens Hotel

Castries–Gros Islet Hwy, Rodney Bay. ☎452-8060, ⊛www.baygardenshotel .com. This is a pleasant place to lay your head if you've been out and about all day, plus it's very good value for the price. Set in bright lemon-lime buildings around an attractive freeform pool and a lushly landscaped courtyard garden, the 71 clean, bright rooms have balconies, TVs, a/c, coffeemakers and minibars; some have kitchenettes. All the rooms are nice, but those on the second floor overlooking the pool and Jacuzzi have the best views. There is a decent if uninspired poolside restaurant, and Reduit Beach is just down the road, accessible by a free shuttle or on foot. Doubles $120; suites $170.

Bay Gardens Inn

Castries–Gros Islet Hwy, Rodney Bay ☎452-8200, ⊛www.baygardensinn .com. Located across the street from its sister hotel, whose pool is open to guests, the *Inn* is smaller, less expensive and slightly more work-a-day, geared toward business travellers rather than holiday-makers. There are about thirty comfortable, attractively decorated rooms with balconies or patios built on two storeys around a small, unadorned courtyard swimming pool; an indoor dining room is plain but serviceable and there's Internet access, a day spa and a hair salon. Doubles $105; studio apartments $125.

Bay Guesthouse

Bay St, Gros Islet ☎450-8956, ⊛www.bay-guesthouse.com. Right on Gros Islet's public beach, this place is within walking distance of Friday night's Jump Up street party. Adequate standard double rooms and studios with kitchens are available at this small guesthouse. No credit cards. Double $35; studios $45.

Caribbean Jewel

Rodney Bay Village ☎452-9199, ⊛www.caribbeanjewelresort.com. Rooms are comfortable if unexceptional, with a/c and TV, plus there's a pool, an onsite restaurant and a beautiful view of the bay. Perched slightly uphill, this is a bit of a walk (ten minutes) to the beach. And while the place is nice enough, there are better choices in this price range. Doubles $110; suites $130.

Coco Kreole

Reduit Beach Drive, Rodney Bay Village ☎452-0712, ⊛www.coco-resorts.com.

▲ COCO PALM

This small, centrally located boutique hotel has twenty rooms, each with a refrigerator, CD player, a/c, cable TV, refrigerator, and in-room safe. There is a patio and a small but attractive swimming pool, plus wireless Internet access is available. Guests have signing privileges at four nearby restaurants, including *Café Claude* next door (see p.77), as well as use of the larger pool and other amenities at the more upscale *Coco Palm* hotel on the adjoining property. A minimum stay of four days is required during peak periods. Continental breakfast is included in the rates. $95.

Coco Palm

Rodney Bay Village ☏ 456-2800, ⊛ www.coco-resorts.com. Designed in accordance with the principles of feng shui, this relaxed but sophisticated four-storey hotel is tucked up against one of the low hills surrounding Rodney Bay. Though set slightly back from the bustle of the main drag, it's still within a couple of minutes' walk from the beach and restaurants. The architecture features steeply gabled windows and double French doors, which open onto narrow balconies overlooking a large sculpted pool. The 71 guestrooms and twelve suites are richly furnished with mahogany French colonial-style pieces, luxurious linens and a soft palette of greens, yellows or blues, as well as all the modern conveniences. Six doubles are "swim-up" rooms with patios that open directly onto the water at a secluded end of the pool. There is an inviting and sophisticated restaurant and bar on-site, as well as a spa and children's Montessori day camp (Jun–Aug); day care and babysitting are available year-round. Doubles $150; suites $225.

Ginger Lily

Reduit Beach Drive, Rodney Bay Village ☏ 458-0300, ⊛ www .thegingerlilyhotel.com. This intimate courtyard hotel, set in a lush garden shaded by mature trees, has eleven attractive rooms done up in dark lacquered rattan, yellow walls and white tile floors. Each room has a TV, refrigerator and sitting area, as well as a quiet, secluded patio with a hammock. Internet access is available, and there is a freshwater pool as well as a small patio restaurant serving three meals a day. Rates include breakfast. Doubles $140; suites $190.

Glencastle Resort

Massade, Gros Islet ☎450-0833, ⊛www.glencastleresort.net. Set on a hill above Gros Islet, this small peachy pink cement fortress just off the main highway has views of Rodney Bay and its marina. The serviceable rooms feature balconies, a/c and cable TV. Though a bit lifeless and tattered, it's relatively inexpensive and convenient for excursions to west coast beaches and the Gros Islet Jump Up (see p.71). $95.

Harmony Marina Suites

Rodney Bay Village ☎452-8756 or 452-0336, ⊛www.harmonysuites.com. One of the original hotels on Rodney Bay's marina, this place is showing its age a bit. The thirty bland but comfortable suites (some carpeted, some with tiled floors) have fridges, coffeemakers and hair dryers, and 22 of them sleep up to four adults; the "premium" suites have kitchenettes and the "luxury" suites overlooking the marina have private sundecks and indoor jacuzzis. There is a restaurant and swimming pool, and the beach is a couple of minutes' walk away. Internet access is available. $120.

Kai Caribe

Rodney Bay Village ☎552-8898. Just a few minutes' walk from Reduit Beach, three beautifully designed and furnished apartments (two one-bedroom and one two-bedroom) share a swimming pool overlooking the marina. With its fully equipped kitchens, this is an excellent choice for those wanting self-catering accommodation in the centre of things. $83.

La Panache Guesthouse

Cas-en-Bas Rd, Gros Islet ☎450-0765, ⊛www.lapanache.com. Built into a steep hillside, you'll find a fantastic view of Rodney Bay harbour at La Panache, with three colourful, simple but homely cottage units. All have private baths, kitchenettes, mosquito nets, fans and a shared balcony. There's a photograph-festooned bar and restaurant (see p.79) offering excellent weekly Wednesday night feasts; a gazebo-style lounge with TV and books to borrow; and Cas-en-Bas beach is only around 1500m to the east. Double $45; apartment $65.

Mango Sands

Reduit Beach Drive ☎452-9800, ⊛www.roomsstlucia.com. Each of the two tidy and cheerful twin-bedded rooms has a private balcony, a/c and a mini-fridge. A minimum three-night stay is required. The *Razmataz Tandoori* restaurant is adjacent. $85.

MJI Villas

Rodney Bay Heights ☎452-8090, ⊛www.mjivilla.com. Set in a residential neighbourhood, these pleasant doubles, studios and two-bedroom apartments – with TV, a/c and balconies or patios overlooking a shared swimming pool – are a fifteen-minute walk from the beach. Doubles $70; studios $90; two-bedroom apartments $125.

Papillon by Rex

Reduit Beach ☎452-0984, ⊛www.rexresorts.com. Guest rooms are serviceable if slightly dated at the all-inclusive *Papillon*. The restaurant offers mediocre buffet meals, but you do have the option of eating at other Rex restaurants at a discount. The main draw here is the beachfront setting. A minimum three-night stay is required. $314.

Royal by Rex

Reduit Beach ☏452-9999, ⓦwww
.rexresorts.com. The *Royal* is
the poshest of the three Rex
Resorts that sit side-by-side
on Reduit Beach. It features
a marble-and-gilt lobby, two
formal dining rooms, a spa
and almost one hundred suites,
each with a balcony or patio.
The rooms are comfortably
if unimaginatively decorated,
and include all the modern
conveniences; walls dividing
the small sitting room from
the bedroom make them feel
rather cramped, however.
The pool – with bridges,
a waterfall and a swim-up
bar – is the centrepiece of
the property, but the most
appealing aspects here are
the beachfront setting and
easy access to the numerous
restaurants across the street.
Though it's not an all-inclusive
resort, meal plans are available.
A minimum three-night stay is
required. $330.

St Lucian by Rex

Reduit Beach ☏452-4351, ⓦwww
.rexresorts.com. This all-inclusive
beachside resort offers sizeable
if sterile rooms with all the
amenities, plus two buffet-
style restaurants, a couple of
bars, tennis and watersports. A
minimum three-night stay is
required. $219.

Stephanie's Hotel

Castries–Gros Islet Hwy, Massade
☏450-8689, ⓦwww.geocities.com
/bb_hotel. Though a bit noisy,
being located on the east side
of the busy Castries–Gros
Islet Highway, this hotel is
convenient for exploring
Rodney Bay. Some of the
twenty rooms have kitchenettes,
and there's a small lobby with
a TV as well as an inexpensive

local bar/restaurant/pizza joint
on the ground floor. $40.

Village Inn and Spa

Reduit Beach Drive ☏458-3300,
ⓦwww.villageinnstlucia.com. The
nearly eighty guestrooms at this
spot, across the street from the
public beach, are built around a
courtyard featuring a pool and
a Jacuzzi. There is a pleasant on-
site restaurant, and rates include
breakfast. Doubles $140, suites
$200.

Villa Zandoli

Rodney Bay ☏452-8898, ⓦwww
.saintelucie.com. This brightly
painted guesthouse is set in
a lush garden on a quiet side
street. The five guestrooms
– some ensuite and some with
shared bath – are cheery, large
and scrupulously clean, plus
there's a communal sitting room,
a library, a barbecue and a well-
equipped kitchen. Free Internet
access is also available, and rates
include continental breakfast.
$63.

Restaurants

Big Chef Steakhouse

Rodney Bay ☏450-0210. Closed Sun.
The popular local-TV chef here
caters to those who like their
(moderately priced) meat. From
an 8oz tenderloin to "as big as
you can handle" (65oz is the
latest record), these steaks are
not for the faint hearted. Pasta
and seafood are available, if you
prefer.

Breadbasket

Rodney Bay Marina ☏452-0647.
Mon–Sat 7am–5pm, Sun and holidays
7am–noon. This sunny little
bakery sits on a wood plank-
covered deck overlooking the
marina. Offerings include tasty

and inexpensive breakfasts (EC$12–15), sandwiches (EC$6–15), burgers and rotis (EC$6–10) as well as pastries and fresh bread.

Buzz

Reduit Beach Drive, Rodney Bay ☏458-0450, 🖳www.buzzstlucia.com. Open for dinner only. Closed Mon. This deservedly popular seafood restaurant has an imaginative menu that features dishes like seafood Creole stew with jumbo shrimp, fresh fish and squid; snapper or tuna baked in a potato crust with tomato basil sauce; a spicy West Indian pepperpot of lamb and beef; and lobster and crabcake supreme with rémoulade sauce for an appetizer. Dessert includes frozen coconut mousse or banana pecan bread pudding with a warm rum sauce, among other sweet delights. The small, stylish dining area opens onto a garden, where there are more tables under the stars. Appetizers average EC$15–30, and mains are EC$32–78.

Café Claude

Reduit Beach Drive, Rodney Bay ☏458-0847. Mon–Thurs 8am–midnight, Fri & Sat 8am–2am, Sun 8am–noon. Casual but sophisticated, this very attractive bistro with a cosy bar offers dining on a deep timbered verandah shaded by lush greenery and appointed with comfortably cushioned teak furniture. Beautifully presented dishes include a saltfish omelette for breakfast (EC$16); local pumpkin soup with garlic bread (EC$16) or smoked salmon and cream-cheese salad (EC$35) for lunch; and coconut chicken curry (EC$40), pan-fried mahi mahi (EC$55) or pumpkin ravioli (EC$39) for dinner. Round out

the meal with St Lucian key lime pie or banana flambé.

Café Olé

Rodney Bay Marina. Mon–Sat 7am–7pm, Sun 8am–11pm. A cheerful, polished hole-in-the-wall café and bar serving gourmet coffees, home-made Italian gelato, salads and sandwiches made with fresh crusty baguettes (EC$9–12). Seating is on a covered wooden deck overlooking the harbour.

Captain's Cellar Pub

Pigeon Island, near Interpretive Centre, Gros Islet ☏450-0918. Mon–Fri 9am–9.30pm, Sat 9am–5pm, Sun 10am–9.30pm. An atmospheric, cavernous, traditional "English" pub housed in a 250-year-old building. There's a wide selection of inexpensive grub – from scrambled eggs and bacon to baked potatoes, salads and main dishes like chilli and risotto. Barbecue is available on Saturday nights (7–9pm) and you can try your hand at darts and skittles.

The Cat's Whiskers

Reduit Beach Drive, Rodney Bay ☏452-8880. Tues–Sun 8am–late. Unassuming pub-restaurant serving moderately priced hearty traditional English fare from full breakfasts to Ploughman's lunches, bangers and mash, hand-cut chips and steak and kidney pies (all from EC$30 to $40); hard cider (EC$8) is available and decent brews on are on tap (EC$10). The popular Sunday brunch (EC$45) is a feast: roast beef, Yorkshire pudding and all the trimmings.

Charthouse

Rodney Bay Marina ☏452-8115. Daily 6–10.30pm. At this dark-wood, waterside restaurant (reserve

▲ THE DOG HOUSE

seats on the deck), steaks, hickory-smoked ribs and lobster are the specialities, with large portions and hearty sides (there's little to nothing of interest on offer here for vegetarians). Top off your meal with a Cuban cigar, which you can buy here.

The Dog House

Rodney Bay ☎452-0054. Daily for lunch and dinner. Tex-Mex food is served to the sounds of Shania Twain and Conway Twitty at *The Dog House*, which is notable mainly as an example of St Lucia's incongruous fondness for American country and western music.

Eagles Inn

Reduit Beach Drive ☎452-0650. Daily 7.30am–midnight; Fri & Sat to 1am. Up against the Rodney Bay Marina channel at the far end of Reduit Beach Drive, this pleasant and casual open-air seafood restaurant has a view of Pigeon Island and Gros Islet village. It specializes in grilled and barbecued seafood, chicken and ribs, including local delicacies such as garlic whelks sauteed with fresh seasonings (EC$25); conch steak creole; or a vegetarian platter of local produce (EC$25). Mains run EC$28–40.

Elena's Italian Ice Cream and Coffee Shop

Rodney Bay ☎458-0576. Daily 10am–11pm. A nice, inexpensive place for a pitstop, with tables on a shady roofed patio on a sidestreet near the beach. Serves various hot and iced coffees, soft drinks, cakes and over a dozen flavours of freshly made ice cream, including grapefruit sorbet and lime sorbet with vodka.

Emeralds Restaurant and Cocktail Lounge

In the *Village Inn*, Reduit Beach Drive ☎458-3300. Open for breakfast and dinner. One of the nicer formal hotel dining rooms in Rodney

▼ EMERALDS RESTAURANT AND COCKTAIL LOUNGE

Bay, with an elaborate, seafood-heavy menu. A three-course dinner averages about EC$100.

Grill and Chill

Reduit Beach Drive, Rodney Bay Village ☎458-4017. Daily breakfast, lunch and dinner. Live music Friday nights. Casual dining with friendly service is offered on the colourful verandah or at a few tables inside. The flavourful menu features traditional St Lucian seafood and meat dishes (EC$25–80, with the average around $30-40) as well as burgers (EC$25–35) and lots of vegetarian options (EC$25–35). Breakfast (EC$25) is available all day.

Jambe de Bois

Pigeon Island, Gros Islet ☎450-8166. Daily 9am–5pm. This simple, inexpensive lunch place with a pleasant waterfront setting serves Creole shrimp and chicken, fish and chips and burgers and sandwiches.

Key Largo

Castries–Gros Islet Hwy, at Rodney Bay ☎452-0282. Daily 9am–11pm. This place across from the marina on the east side of the Castries–Gros Islet Highway serves by far the best pizza on the island, freshly baked in a wood-fired brick oven and moderately priced; excellent pasta dishes are also available. Be warned, though – meals may be accompanied by pumping music from the sports gym upstairs.

La Panache

Cas-en-Bas Rd, Gros Islet ☎450-0765. Open Wednesday evenings; call by Monday for reservations. Once a week, the proprietors of La Panache lay on one of the island's best dining experiences: an informal Creole buffet featuring at least ten different West Indian dishes, served alfresco on a roofed terrace overlooking the garden. The moderately priced menu is built around fresh fish, poultry and seasonally available market veggies, and dishes are passed around family-style.

La Trattoria del Mare

Rodney Bay ☎458-0333. Lunch noon–3pm, dinner 6.30–10.30pm. Closed Mon. Reservations recommended. Fine Italian cuisine is served in a cosy, candlelit setting. A skewer of squid costs EC$45 and seafood, chicken and pasta dishes run from EC$42 to $54.

The Lime

Reduit Beach Drive, Rodney Bay ☎452-0761. Wed–Mon 11am–midnight. "Liming" is West Indian slang for "hanging out", and this is one of Rodney Bay's more popular spots to do just that. The food is consistently good Caribbean fare, with especially tasty rotis (EC$10–15, although most of the other dishes start at EC$35). Dining is indoors and alfresco, and an in-house DJ provides music nightly.

Memories of Hong Kong

Reduit Beach Drive, Rodney Bay ☎452-8218. Mon–Sat 4.30pm–late. Very good traditional Cantonese cuisine is the main draw here, the island's only open-kitchen restaurant.

Razmataz Tandoori

Reduit Beach Drive ☎452-9800, ⊛www.razmatazstlucia.com. Wed–Mon 4pm–late. If you're craving curry, then this popular restaurant is a good bet. Specialities are spicy vindaloo, korma and tikka

▲ SCUTTLEBUTT'S BAR AND INN

masala, all prepared with tandoori (grilled) chicken, lamb, beef or shrimp; there are plenty of vegetarian options as well. The Indian fabrics, candles and rich colours complement the food nicely, plus there is occasional live music. Starters average EC$20; mains run EC$29–59; vegetable side dishes are EC$22 and Indian sweets cost EC$15–18.

Red Snapper

Rodney Bay, ☏ 466-8377. Wed–Sun 5pm–late. A popular multi-storey, middle-of-the-road restaurant catering to seafood aficionados with a handful of options for both vegetarians (the usual pasta primavera) and carnivores (barbecued or curried chicken). Appetizers include garlic bread, crab cakes and scallop fritters (EC$7– EC$18), while a bread boat filled with seafood snacks is EC$30; entrees include the fish of the day (EC$50), coconut curried chicken (EC$45), vegetable pasta (EC$38) and burgers (EC$20).

Scuttlebutt's Bar and Grill

Rodney Bay Marina ☏ 452-0351. Daily from 7:30am for breakfast, lunch, dinner and drinks. A great, casual hangout with a large, open-air stone and timber-roofed dining area overlooking Rodney Bay harbour and the green hills beyond. Breakfast (around EC$30) is English-style with eggs and bacon or Lucian-style with saltfish, bakes (heavy soda bread) and cocoa tea. For lunch (EC$20–40), choose from soups, salads, sandwiches or fish and chips in beer batter. Supper dishes (EC$20–40) include curried chicken, coconut shrimp and pasta, with banana flambé drenched in dark rum (EC$12) for dessert. There's a pool table, a reading nook and hammocks for hanging out.

Sabrina's Beach Bar

Reduit Beach. Daily for lunch. This beachside snack bar dishes up

▼ STEEL BAND AT SPINNAKERS

cheap and filling St Lucian specialities such as rotis and boullion (a thin stew of lentils, meat and dumplings), as well as cold beer and soft drinks.

Spinnakers

Reduit Beach ☎ 452-8491. Daily 9am–11pm. With a prime beachfront location, this hopping bar and restaurant has a view of Pigeon Island and the sunset. Serves a mix of steaks, grilled seafood and burgers with a family-friendly kids' menu; most dishes hover around EC$20. Local lobster is the most popular and expensive item listed (EC$85), but the ribs are tangy, tender and a third of the price. A steel band plays on Sun from noon to 3pm.

Triangle Pub

Reduit Beach Drive ☎ 452-0334. Daily 8am–late. At this cheap and cheerful grill, the chefs will happily barbecue everything but your socks. And they do it well, with all the trimmings. No credit cards, but with an average cost of EC$12 per meal, you probably won't be needing one.

Bars and clubs

Charlie's

Rodney Bay Village ☎ 458-0565. *Charlie's* is the place to be any night of the week, with a piano bar Tues, Wed and Sun, a DJ the rest of the week and dancing to a wide variety of music at the adjoining nightclub Wed–Sat (an EC$20 cover is charged on Fri & Sat). Tues is Karaoke night as well (beginning at 6pm), led by a local with strong vocals.

The Lime

Reduit Beach Drive, Rodney Bay Village ☎ 452-0761. Closed Tues. *The Lime*, with an in-house DJ, features a wide range of music and is one of the island's most popular nightlife venues.

The Red Room

At the Blue Martini, Reduit Beach Drive. Features live music on weekends, including acoustic alternative from time to time.

Rumours

Rodney Bay Village ☎ 452-9249. Across the street from *Charlie's* and popular with an upmarket crowd, *Rumours* has live music or a DJ on Fri and Sat (EC$10 after 11pm), plus Retro Tuesdays, Salsa Wednesdays and Karaoke Thursdays. A backyard wooden deck is used for dancing under the stars. Daily from 9pm.

Triangle Pub

Rodney Bay Village. Open daily until late. This small barbecue next to *The Lime* hosts live music on occasion, from reggae and steel bands to jazz. The main entertainment, however, is Karaoke on Mon, Thurs, Sat and Sun. Come for the good fun, good mix of people and good cheap food.

The northern tip and the northeast coast

Immediately north of bustling Rodney Bay and the densely populated community of Gros Islet, the geography and character of the island changes noticeably. The area's main road climbs up into the northern tip's chichi hilltop residential community of Cap Estate, winding past palatial villas surrounded by well-tended lawns and gardens, through St Lucia's only golf course, and by a couple of small hotels and secluded beaches.

In contrast, the northeastern coast is virtually wild and largely undeveloped. It is a bit of challenge to reach – 4WD is necessary to negotiate the steep, rough tracks leading to the coast, most of which are not signposted or mapped. But the rewards are the spectacular panoramic views from Pointe Hardy; an inspired hike along the picturesque coastal walking path from Cas-en-Bas Beach; and relaxation along the long, lonely beach at Grand Anse, where giant leatherback turtles migrate to lay their eggs each spring.

Cap Estate

This conspicuously upscale residential area is distinguished by large villas and estates dotting the hills east of the highway. It's home to the St Lucia Golf and Country Club, the island's only eighteen-hole public golf course.

Smuggler's Cove

If you're after an ocean swim and some goodsnorkelling, head for Smuggler's Cove, a small, protected spot edged with brown sugary sand and backed by tall, sheltering cliffs. On the northestern shore of Cap Estate, Smuggler's Cove can be accessed from the main road, past the

▼ CAP ESTATE

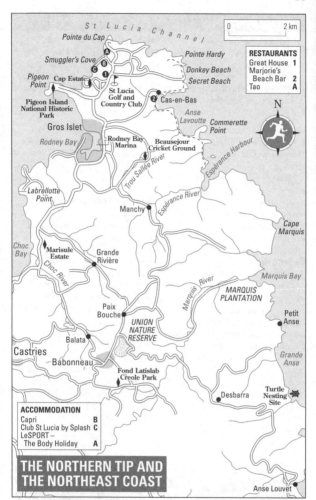

RESTAURANTS
Great House 1
Marjorie's
  Beach Bar 2
Tao A

ACCOMMODATION
Capri B
Club St Lucia by Splash C
LeSPORT –
  The Body Holiday A

**THE NORTHERN TIP AND
THE NORTHEAST COAST**

exclusive *LeSPORT* resort
(see p.88). Make sure to bring
your own refreshments, as the
snack shacks here are only open
sporadically.

Pointe du Cap
Pointe du Cap, less than 5km
from Rodney Bay, is the
northernmost point on the island
and has a wild, untended air
along with epic, panoramic views.

Pointe Hardy
From Cap Estate, several dusty,
unmarked dirt roads bear east
to Pointe Hardy, located on
the dry and stoney northeast
Atlantic coast which, in contrast
to the lush greenness of the rest
of the island, is covered with
scrubby acacias, cacti, sisals and
prickly pears. The view from
Pointe Hardy is magnificent,
embracing crashing white

Safety concerns

Visitors to the Atlantic coast north and south of Cas-en-Bas should take utmost care and stay out of the water. These unmarked and unmanned beaches have seen many people – locals and tourists alike – drown, victims of powerful Atlantic undercurrents. There is a new luxury condominium complex under construction at Cas-en-Bas Beach, but for the most part the area is deserted, so tell someone where you are going before you set off.

surf, a cactus-filled valley and scallops of light sand at Donkey Beach and Cas-en-Bas to the south.

Though you're unlikely to encounter one, the area is also home to a non-venomous boa constrictor; dark with black and yellow patches, it is locally known as *tête chien*.

Cas-en-Bas

The small, scattered settlement of Cas-en-Bas, on the undeveloped northeast coast, boasts a wide curve of secluded beach with some shade trees and an outlying reef taming the rougher waters of the ocean. This is one of the few beaches on the Atlantic coast where you'll be able to safely go for a swim – on a calm day.

You can walk the road from Gros Islet to Cas-en-Bas in an hour, which is a much more appealing option than negotiating the endless mucky potholes by 4WD (don't even attempt it after rain, or in a regular car).

Secret Beach and Donkey Beach

The Cas-en-Bas road ends at the ocean, but a particularly isolated spot, Secret Beach, is a ten-minute walk north, along a trail that hugs the rocky, cactus-strewn coastline – look for a track that goes back down to the water, cutting through thick, leafy bushes.

A few more minutes north along the coastal track brings you past an open field to another seapath, along which, after half an hour or so, you'll find a remote spot of honey-coloured sand known as Donkey Beach.

▼ SECRET BEACH

▲ COMERETTE POINT

Anse Lavoutte and Comerette Point

Thirty minutes' walk south of Cas-en-Bas along the unmarked coastal path brings you to Anse Lavoutte, a desolate and little-used beach that makes a good reststop enroute to Comerette Point, which is an hour's walk further along. A green promontory extending into the water, Comerette Point affords a rewarding view up and down the windswept coast.

Grand Anse

The forest hamlet of Desbarra is the gateway to the wide, windswept Grande Anse beach on the Atlantic coast, boasting more than 2km of blonde sand set against a backdrop of cliffs and hills covered with dry vegetation. The long expanse of beach is inviting and usually devoid of visitors, but as strong winds churn up a rough surf, swimming is not advised and many people have died through

recklessness here. The main lure of Grand Anse, though, is the annual visit of sea turtles: the bay is the primary St Lucian nesting spot for endangered leatherbacks, who also lay their eggs on several other beaches around the island, including Fond D'Or, the next bay to the south; Anse Lavoutte to the north; and Anse Mamin on the southwest coast of the island.

Turtle watch

Grande Anse. Watches run daily March–July. US$65. In conjunction with the Department of Fisheries, Heritage Tours (see p.149) organizes an annual programme of turtle watches at Grand Anse, which allow visitors to

▼ GRAND ANSE

The leatherback turtle

The rarest – and the largest – of the sea turtles that frequent Caribbean waters, the **leatherback** (*Dermochelys coriacea*) has a shell as long as 1.5m and a body weight of up to 680kg; a male weighing in at 1144kg is the biggest specimen on record.

Named for their triangular **carapace** or shell, which is covered by a layer of leathery brown-and-black skin rather than the hard scales of other species, leatherback turtles have changed little in their 65 million years of existence. Sadly, they now face **extinction**: leatherbacks are still hunted by humans, and ocean pollution and accidental entrapment in fishing nets have killed thousands. Furthermore, their laying beaches all around the island are being transformed into tourist resorts or diminished by sand mining, and as their main food is **jellyfish**, they often mistake floating plastic waste for food – the immense male mentioned above was found with 24 plastic bags in his intestines.

Nesting females are among the most implacable mothers on earth, leaving the ocean every two to six years only to lay eggs. Under the cover of night, they lumber up the sand and burrow the hole into which they lay around eighty eggs before returning to the sea for about ten days. Females will go through this process up to a dozen times during a laying period, depositing as many as eight hundred eggs during the March to July season. These incubate for as long as three months and produce fully functional hatchlings, which emerge at night and paw their way to the surf. Only about one in a thousand baby leatherbacks survives the six years it takes to reach maturity.

During the leatherback egg-laying season, the beach is closed to the public and volunteers head out to Grande Anse to monitor nesting females and protect the turtles and their eggs from predators and human poachers. You can witness the nesting for yourself by joining one of the turtle watches (see p.85).

experience the stirring spectacle of leatherback turtles laying their eggs. The all-night watches take place daily in leatherback breeding season and the price covers transport from your hotel, overnight accommodation in tents, dinner, breakfast, sleeping mats and a T-shirt; you'll have to bring your own flashlight, toilet paper and warm clothing, as nights can be cool and breezy. Once at the beach, you'll settle into a rustic tent village and take turns patrolling the beach. Whenever a turtle is spotted, you'll be called to have a look. The watches are becoming very popular, so to ensure a place it's best to contact Heritage Tours or the Desbarra Turtlewatch Group (☎284–2812) – the community group that organizes the watch – well in advance.

Babonneau

A small farming community, Babonneau is worth visiting for its views of the steep, heavily-forested ravines and hillsides,

▼ A FIELD NEAR BABONNEAU

Empress Josephine

The birth details of the girl who would become **Empress Josephine**, wife of Napoleon Bonaparte, remain a hotly disputed matter of St Lucian national pride. While locals commonly believe that she was born at a plantation estate called Paix Bouche, near Babonneau, many in neighbouring Martinique claim that she was born on their island. As no birth certificate exists, proof is more a matter of legend than fact. St Lucians will grudgingly acknowledge that Josephine was conceived in Martinique, but assert that she was born here and lived here for seven years before returning to the other island with her family.

Josephine was the daughter of Joseph Tascher de la Pagerie, an estate owner who settled the village of **Babonneau**. In 1779, at the age of 16, she married French military officer and nobleman Alexandre, Vicomte de Beauharnais. Due to his status as a nobleman, Beauharnais was one of many arrested during the French Revolution's Reign of Terror and was subsequently beheaded in 1794. Josephine married Napoleon in 1796 and became empress when he declared himself emperor in 1804. The marriage ended in 1809, when Napoleon divorced her, and she died in 1814. Keeping things in the family, Josephine and Beauharnais's daughter, Hortense, married Napoleon's brother, Louis, and bore him a son, the future emperor Napoleon III.

and for a glimpse into rural St Lucian life. Several rivers flow through the hills around the village, and some people believe that the town's name is a Patois version of the old French phrase *barre bon eau*, meaning, roughly, "mountain ridge, good water".

While there's not a great deal to see in Babonneau, stop by the large and brightly coloured Catholic church built in 1947 on a hill in the sparsely populated "centre" of the village. Also, a few kilometres inland on the road to Babonneau you'll find the Union Agricultural Centre – an interpretive centre, mini-zoo and hiking trail (see p.134).

Fond Latislab Creole Park

Fond Assor ☏450-6327 or 450-5461. At the village of Fond Assor, a couple of kilometres southeast of Babonneau, Fond Latislab Creole Park is a touristy outdoor museum designed to demonstrate traditional Creole cooking, fishing, saw milling and music. Book a tour directly, or through Heritage Tours (see p.149).

Accommodation

Capri

Smuggler's Cove, Cap Estate ☏450-0009, ☉www.capristlucia.com. This adorable nine-room guesthouse nestled in the hills above Smuggler's Cove is the perfect getaway for travellers who like a feeling of camaraderie. The airy, tastefully appointed rooms all have TV, a/c, and stunning views of the bay; some have balconies with hammocks. Meals are taken together at a long dining table or alfresco on a balcony. Yoga, tai chi and meditation classes are offered on a wooden deck overlooking the pool and herb garden below, and there is an open-air honesty bar and secluded nooks are located around the property. Though it caters primarily to groups (wedding parties, families, etc), individual bookings are accepted as well. For groups of 1 to 8 people, rates are $700 per night and include breakfast.

Club St Lucia by Splash

Becune Bay, Cap Estate ⓣ450-0551, ⓦwww.clubstluciabysplash.com. Purely functional one-storey guestrooms are scattered over several treed acres fronted by a small, attractive curve of light brown sand. This sprawling all-inclusive features several cavernous restaurants, a waterside bar and two swimming pools.Popular with families, this is not the place for individuals seeking solitude and peace. From $165.

LeSPORT – The Body Holiday

Cap Estate ⓣ457-7800 or 1-800/544-2883 (US and Canada) or 0870-220-2344 (UK), ⓦwww.thebodyholiday.com. One of the island's few all-inclusive resorts that manages to escape the family-oriented associations and make singles feel comfortable. On the downside, rooms are somewhat barren and the beach is just adequate, but the emphasis is on getting you out, about and active. The place is usually full of stressed-out city types indulging in the spa treatments, exercise classes, hikes, watersports, golf lessons, archery and tai chi. The food is plentiful, healthful and well-prepared, especially at the restaurant *Tao* (see opposite). From $680.

Restaurants

Great House

Cap Estate ⓣ450-0450. Tea at 4:30pm, happy hour at 5:30, dinner 6:30–10pm. Closed Mon. Fine dining is offered in an old stone plantation house overlooking Becune Bay, with seating inside or on the stone patio. The West Indian and French cuisine (mains run EC$54 to $70) includes oven-roasted pumpkin soup with fried plantains to start (EC$19) followed by shrimps in Creole sauce or fillet of dorado, chicken or duck, with crème brûlée or lime cheese cake for dessert. There is a piano bar on-site and the Derek Walcott amphitheatre, where you can occasionally see local productions, is adjacent.

Marjorie's Restaurant and Bar

Cas-en-Bas Beach. Open for lunch and drinks daily. A rocket booster sits in the front yard of this attractive, inexpensive timber-and-thatch beach bar and grill

▼ GREAT HOUSE

▲ MARJORIE'S RESTAURANT AND BAR

serving St Lucian comfort food such as barbeque chicken and seafood done Creole-style.

Tao

At *LeSPORT*, Cap Estate ☎ 457-7821. Open for dinner daily. Superlative East/West fusion cuisine, impeccable service and a gorgeous setting overlooking the bay make this one of the island's finest dining experiences. Choose from sushi, tofu dishes and wonderful seafood, and don't forget to leave room for dessert. The menu's imaginative combinations include rock melon gazpacho served with fuji apple sorbet or lemongrass chicken salad to start; tamarind lamb or fresh seafood for entrees; and warm, baked chocolate served with mint tea ice cream for dessert. A three course dinner will cost US$30-$60 per person, not including drinks. Advanced booking is essential; request a table on the edge of the balcony.

The west coast

Virtually undeveloped, the 20km or so of coast between Castries and Soufrière is dotted with quiet fishing villages built at the mouths of rivers flowing out of densely forested mountains. The only pocket of low-key tourist activity here is at Marigot Bay, which affords one of the prettiest vistas in the Caribbean. Immediately south of the bay, the area's main road traverses the broad Roseau Valley, once a major sugarcane and banana-growing region, and still home to St Lucia's only rum distillery, as well as the Millet Nature Reserve and Bird Sanctuary, which borders the Roseau River. The road then continues through the quiet fishing villages of Anse La Raye and Canaries, both fronting photogenic coves filled with turquoise water surrounded by steep cliffs. La Sikwi Sugar Mill, on the banks of the Anse La Raye River, and the waterfalls a few kilometres upstream make good destinations for day-trips.

Cul de Sac Valley

Chiselled out by the Cul de Sac River, one of the island's longest, the Cul de Sac Valley's relatively flat and extremely fertile plains make it ideal for farming (the area is abundant with banana fields and small-holdings). The only blight on the landscape is the large,

▼ DOOLITTLE BEACH, MARIGOT BAY

modern Hess Oil plant and its massive shipping docks, as well as the hulking main plant of the island's electricity company, Lucelec. Just past Lucelec you'll find the eastbound turnoff for Dennery and the Barre de L'Isle hiking trail (see p.136).

Marigot Bay

With a clutch of glamorous small hotels and restaurants tucked along the shore and into the steep, green hillsides encircling the waterfront, Marigot Bay is one of the Caribbean's most photographed landscapes. Its classic tropical appeal has even caught the eye of Hollywood in the past – the bay was the setting for the 1967 film *Doctor Dolittle*.

From the coastal highway, the road into Marigot Bay ascends to a lookout point offering memorable views: turquoise water fringed by dense vegetation, with an inviting spit of white sand and palm trees

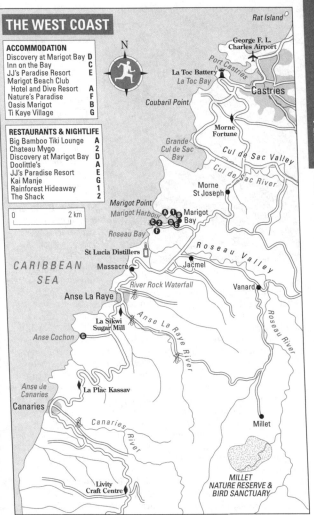

THE WEST COAST

ACCOMMODATION

Discovery at Marigot Bay	D
Inn on the Bay	C
JJ's Paradise Resort	E
Marigot Beach Club Hotel and Dive Resort	A
Nature's Paradise	F
Oasis Marigot	B
Ti Kaye Village	G

RESTAURANTS & NIGHTLIFE

Big Bamboo Tiki Lounge	A
Chateau Mygo	2
Discovery at Marigot Bay	D
Doolittle's	A
JJ's Paradise Resort	E
Kai Manje	G
Rainforest Hideaway	1
The Shack	2

0   2 km

CARIBBEAN SEA

Rat Island

George F. L. Charles Airport

Port Castries

La Toc Battery
La Toc Bay

Castries

Coubaril Point

Morne Fortune

Grande Cul de Sac Bay

Cul de Sac Valley

Cul de Sac River

Morne St Joseph

Marigot Point
Marigot Harbour
Marigot Bay

Roseau Bay

Roseau Valley

St Lucia Distillers

Jacmel

Massacré

River Rock Waterfall

Vanard

Anse La Raye

Anse La Raye River

Roseau River

La Sikwi Sugar Mill

Anse Cochon

Anse de Canaries

La Plàc Kassav

Canaries

Canaries River

Millet

Livity Craft Centre

MILLET NATURE RESERVE & BIRD SANCTUARY

extending into the middle of the bay. Marigot's steep access road then descends the hill for about 1km, ending abruptly at the compact waterfront. To the right is the ever-crowded jetty of The Moorings Yacht Charters (☎451-4357, ⊛www.moorings .com) and the new luxury resort *Discovery* (see p.95); clustered around the wharf are the small police station, a customs and immigration office for incoming yachts (☎452-3487) and a taxi stand (☎453-4406). The entrances to the brace of small hotels are set a few metres back from the

▲ BANANA FIELD, ROSEAU VALLEY

lowlands valley south of Marigot Bay. Near the distillery, but situated a few kilometres off the main road on the inland side, the church in the village of Jacmel boasts some fine *omeros* murals of the black madonna, painted by one of St Lucia's most respected artists, Dunstan St Omer.

St Lucia Distillers

☎ 451-4258, 🌐 www .sludistillers.com/tour. Daily 9am–3pm. US $10. The island's only remaining rum distillery, St Lucia Distillers (est. 1922) is a major local employer, with a staff of around three hundred. Touristy but fun, its "Rhythm of Rum Tour"(call ahead to make reservations) takes you through the distillery, where the liquor's history is explained through a short video, photo displays, mannequins dressed as plantation workers and a tasting session. Sunlink Tours (see p.148) covers an excursion here in conjunction with their trip to Marigot Bay (US$40).

Millet Bird Sanctuary

Millet ☎ 451-1691. Mon–Fri 8.30am– 3pm. Nature Trail EC$25/US$10; guided birdwatching hike EC$75/ US$30 (book 24 hours in advance). Over thirty species of birds live in this sanctuary, including five found only on St Lucia (such as the St Lucia Black Finch, with its thick black beak, and the St Lucia Parrot, boasting a bright green, blue and red coat). A scenic 2.8km loop trail affords views into the rainforest

waterfront, high in the hills overlooking the bay.

Though a sign above the water taxi jetty straight ahead at the end of the road reads "Welcome to the Marigot Beach Club," the club and its palm-tree shaded beach (the only beach in the immediate area) are actually a few hundred metres across the bay, accessible 24 hours a day via a two-minute ferry ride (EC$5 round trip). Slung along a short and thin promontory that juts into the bay from the hotel restaurant, the beach is nonetheless spacious, with calm surf, plenty of shade and good snorkelling to its west side. Non-guests are welcome to use the hotel beach and watersports concession, provided they buy at least a soft drink at the hotel's waterfront restaurant.

Roseau Valley

Dotted with small settlements and planted with banana fields, Roseau, home to St Lucia's largest rum distillery, is a fertile and of both Morne Gimie (the highest peak on St Lucia) and the Roseau Dam. The trail takes about two hours to cover on your own; alternatively, a four-hour guided birdwatching tour is also available.

Anse La Raye

Anse La Raye's few quiet, narrow streets are lined with weatherbeaten wooden cottages, unassuming rum shops where locals play dominoes and fishing shacks draped with drying nets. Its beach fronts a broad bay that's littered with brightly painted fishing boats; you might also see fishermen hauling in the flat, long-tailed skate after which the village is named.

Spurred on by the popularity of the Jump Up in Gros Islet (see p.71), Anse La Raye hosts a fish fry every Friday night. It's a much smaller affair than its northern counterpart, with more emphasis on eating and drinking at big communal tables in the main street than going crazy until the wee hours. The variety of seafood – from lobster and titiri to lambi and dolphin – is more expansive and expensive than in Gros Islet, but

at EC$10 for a char-grilled tuna steak, some corn, a hot bake and a large rum and coke, it's still cheaper (and more fun) than anything else around.

As you enter Anse la Raye from the north, a rough dirt road on the left at the bottom of the hill leads to the fifteen-metre manmade River Rock Waterfall (EC$5). You can swim at the base of the cascade, and there are picnic tables, a changing area and a bar serving beer and soft drinks as well. Because it's pretty far off the beaten track, you'll probably only have to share the place with a few locals – if you don't have it all to yourself.

La Sikwi Sugar Mill

Anse La Raye ☎ 452-6323 or 451-4245. Daily 9am–3.00pm. US$5.
On the banks of the Anse La Raye River, La Sikwi Sugar Mill (La Sikwi means sugar in Creole) was one of the few British-owned sugar mills on St Lucia, built in 1876 to process sugarcane grown on the surrounding plantation. Today the plantation exports flowers and cocoa, and the stone ruins of the sugar mill

▼ ANSE LA RAYE

▲ CANARIES

are picturesque, surrounded by beautifully tended flower gardens. There are a few artefacts and some fascinating historical photographs on display, plus guided tours and an atmospheric bar and restaurant. Sunlink Tours (see p.148) combines a visit to the mill with a swim and photo op at the Anse La Raye Waterfalls, situated about 3km upriver.

On an unnamed road, the mill is difficult to find. Heading south on the main road through Anse La Raye village, turn left at the junction opposite the phone booth (the last junction before you cross the bridge heading out of town). You will come to a "Y" junction after a few metres along this road. Take the road on the right, past the school. A few hundred metres further on will bring you to the gate of La Sikwi, on your right. You will have to park on the side on the road, which runs alongside the river.

Anse La Raye Waterfalls

From La Sikwi Sugar Mill, if you continue inland on the road that follows the river for a further 3km or so (a 4WD is necessary, or you can walk),

you'll reach the picturesque Anse La Raye Waterfalls – a nice spot for a picnic and a dip in the pool below the falls.

Anse Cochon

The secluded beach at Anse Cochon – accessible from *Ti Kaye Village Resort* (see p.96) or by water taxi from Soufrière – is one of the most attractive on St Lucia, with a thick sweep of tree-backed sand. There's a small bar and restaurant at one end, where you can rent snorkelling gear.

La Plac Kassav

In a low, unpainted wooden building almost 2km north of Canaries, La Plac Kassav bakery sells freshly made cassava bread – soft, dense rounds prepared using a traditional Creole recipe (EC$6 each). For US$1, you can watch the baking process, which includes pounding the cassava roots to make the flour and cooking the dough over a wood fire.

Canaries

There is a great scenic viewing point at the top of the hill as you climb up out of the small fishing community of Canaries on the south side. From here you can see the village laid out before you, the turquoise bay dotted with bobbing multi-coloured fishing boats and the Canaries River as it winds its way to the sea. South of town you'll find six or so waterfalls along the river. Forest rangers might be persuaded to act as guides, though the simplest way to find someone to take you there is to ask around town (you'll pay at least US$25 per person).

Livity Craft Centre

A woodcarving studio about seven kilometres south of Canaries, Livity Craft Centre is well-stocked with authentic local sculpture and artwork, including functional items like clay pots and basketry as well as fine art. A giftshop is attached.

Accommodation

Discovery at Marigot Bay

Marigot Bay ☎458-5300, ☻www .sonesta.com/stlucia. The construction of this 124-unit luxury resort on the south side of Marigot Bay (due to be finished in 2006) has altered the atmosphere and landscape of this sleepy little cove. The 67 rooms and 57 suites are elegantly furnished in dark wood and fine white linens, with flatscreen TVs, DVD players, refrigerators and coffeemakers. Some of the suites have private plunge pools and kitchens. In addition, there are expected to be numerous bars and restaurants, two swimming pools, boutiques, a bank, a grocery and a marina. Rates include a welcome drink, a fifteen-minute massage and daily yoga classes. Doubles $220, suites $420.

Inn on the Bay

South side of Marigot Bay ☎451-4260, ☻www.saint-lucia.com. In a secluded hilltop setting overlooking the south side of the bay, this pleasant five-room guesthouse offers a relaxing getaway. Bright and airy rooms open onto the deck and pool, and a free shuttle takes you to the beach and restaurants around Marigot Bay. Alternatively, if you're keen on getting some exercise, you can take the three hundred steps down to a private beach. The hosts are extremely knowledgeable about the island, and the sea breeze wafting up the hill renders a/c unnecessary while also discouraging the mosquitoes. Continental breakfast is included, and wireless Internet access is available. $155.

JJ's Paradise Resort

Marigot Bay ☎451-4076, ☻www .jj-paradise.com. Despite its name, this is not a resort. Instead, cosy wooden bungalows just a two-minute water-taxi ride from the beach are set in a shady garden at the edge of a mangrove thicket. Rates include breakfast, and kids under twelve stay for free. You can reach *JJ's* by taking the drive on the right at the lookout at the top of the hill. $150.

Marigot Beach Club Hotel and Dive Resort

North side of Marigot Bay ☎451-4974, ☻www.marigotbeachclubhotel.com, ☻www.marigotdiveresort.com. One of the most appealing resorts on St Lucia, the *Beach Club* has a relaxed holiday vibe enhanced by its idyllic setting on a sandy spit of land dotted with tall palms. The lovely 25 guest rooms, studio apartments and villas feature terracotta

▲ MANGROVE SWAMP, JJ'S PARADISE RESORT

floors, four-poster beds, gauzy white curtains, fresh flowers and double french doors opening onto deep balconies overlooking the beach and the bay. All rooms include kitchenettes, TVs, CD players, a/c, phones and wireless Internet access; there's also a gym, a swimming pool, watersports (such as kayaking, diving and snorkelling) and two charming bayside restaurants. Rates include breakfast. Studios $184, rooms $168, one-bedroom villa $197.

Nature's Paradise

South side of Marigot Bay ☎458-3550, ⊛www.stluciaparadise.com. Two one-bedroom cottages are perched high above the bay in an extravagantly lush garden complete with a waterfall-fed pool. Each nicely furnished unit has a kitchenette, glass block shower and deep, private balcony with a sea view. The owner conducts daily stretching and tai chi classes, and rates include breakfast every day except Sunday. $145.

Oasis Marigot

Marigot Bay ☎1-800/263-4204 (US & Canada) or 00-800/2785-8241 (UK & worldwide), ⊛www.oasismarigot.com. Nestled in the hills on both shores of the bay, all of the villas, cottages and apartments here have great views, balconies and full kitchens; some have swimming pools, chefs and chauffeurs. Villas from $189, cottages from $215, apartments from $305.

Ti Kaye Village

Anse Cochon ☎456-8101, ⊛www .tikaye.com. The remote location overlooking Anse Cochon helps make this the island's most secluded and romantic haven. A clutch of spacious wooden cottages with gingerbread trim are tucked discreetly into the hillside. Rooms have large four-poster beds; outdoor showers in private grottos edged with bamboo; and deep, cosy verandahs with double-size hammocks. You can dine in the relaxed but elegant restaurant (see p.98), and an excellent full breakfast is included in the rates. Scuba diving and a full range of other activities are available. No children under twelve are permitted. $250.

Restaurants

Big Bamboo Tiki Lounge

North side of Marigot Bay, at Marigot Beach Club ☎451-4974.

TI KAYE VILLAGE

Open for dinner and drinks. This atmospheric, torch-lit thatched lodge situated over the water offers a Polynesian menu and colourful tropical cocktails.

Chateau Mygo

North side of Marigot Bay ☎451-4772, ⊛www.chateaumygo.com. Daily 7am–11pm. A simple but appealing restaurant at the end of the Marigot Bay road that serves three meals daily (main dishes are EC$20–30). The cuisine is very much Creole style, with lots of seafood and local produce, plus there are thin-crust pizzas and tropical cocktails. Seating is on a covered pier on the water's edge. Dinner reservations are recommended.

Discovery at Marigot Bay

South side of Marigot Bay ☎458-5300, ⊛www.sonesta.com/stlucia. You can enjoy breakfast, lunch and dinner at *The Boudreau Restaurant*, which overlooks the bay, or breakfast, lunch or all-day snacks at *The Coffee Dock*, offering outdoor seating on a dock. *The Doubloon Restaurant* is a casual spot at the marina, and *The Bakery* features all sorts of crumbly goods as well as ice cream.

Doolittle's

North side of Marigot Bay, at *Marigot Beach Club* ☎451-4974, ⊛www .marigotdiveresort.com. Hearty breakfasts and Caribbean-fusion lunches and dinners are served in this lively open-air spot built over the water. There is a friendly, casual bar, as well as comfy sofas for lounging, books and newspapers for perusing, pool tables and board games, a BBQ on Saturday nights and live music Tues–Sun. The menu features spicy shrimp tikka, salads and crab cakes for appetizers (EC$12–36); pasta dishes (EC$25–49); seafood (EC$50-95); and Caribbean-style chicken or beef (EC$55).

JJ's Paradise Resort

East end of Marigot Bay ☎451-4076, ⊛www.jj-paradise.com. Daily 8am–late. Choose between a nightly buffet in a big, covered dining room overlooking the parking lot, or an à la carte menu in the waterfront seating area, reached by a short stroll along a wooden boardwalk through a mangrove thicket. Lively Wednesday

▲ RAINFOREST HIDEAWAY

Creole crab nights are popular with locals, and Saturday BBQs feature pork, ribs, chicken and fish. Pizzas are available Tues–Sun.

Kai Manje

Ti Kaye Village Resort, Anse Cochon ☎456-8101, ⊛www.tikaye.com. Three meals a day are served on a candlelit canopied terrace that faces the sea. Breakfast is a buffet of fresh fruits, pastries, eggs and cooked meats, and lunch features a selection of delicious salads, sandwiches, fish, poultry or pasta dishes. The daily-changing dinner menu, cooked to perfection, may include gazpacho spiked with vodka or saltfish accra for starters (US$4); fillet steak or poached grouper served with basmati rice and grated vegetables for entrees (US$22–24); and baked vanilla cheesecake for dessert (US$6).

Rainforest Hideaway

North side of Marigot Bay ☎451-4485 or 286-0511. Mon & Wed–Sat noon–3pm & 6–10pm, Sun noon–10pm. This intimate floating champagne bar and restaurant features an imaginative menu that changes daily, plus live entertainment three or four nights a week. With soft jazz and candlelit tables, this is a very romantic setting in which you can enjoy upscale meals like roast duck with Roquefort sauce and toasted pecans followed by ginger-rubbed red snapper with Earl Grey rice and a coconut and coriander cream sauce; dessert choices may include a honey-glazed banana tart. No children are allowed after 6pm, reservations are strongly recommended, and you are expected to dress the part (ie no beachwear). Mains cost EC$60–90.

The Shack

Marigot Bay ☎451-4145. Daily 9am–11pm; breakfast items on request; happy hour 5–7pm. Sitting out over the water on stilts, this casual and moderately priced café-restaurant has an open-air verandah that makes it a great place to relax and take in the view. Deliciously prepared sandwiches and salads are available at lunchtime, and the Caribbean/American dinner menu features lots of super-fresh seafood – the kingfish burgers, conch fritters and mahi mahi are very popular.

Bars and clubs

JJ's Paradise Resort

East end of Marigot Bay ☎451-4076. Wed and Fri & Sat, open late. This simple, wooden, hotel bar on the waterfront is a local hotspot; Wednesday is ladies' night.

Marigot Bay Beach Club

North side of Marigot Bay ☎451-4974. The liveliest spots in Marigot Bay's limited nightlife scene are at *Marigot Bay Beach Club*. The relaxed beachside bar *Doolittle's* features pool tables, comfy nooks and live music most nights, and the cosy, torchlit *Big Bamboo Lounge* sits out over the water a few steps away.

Rainforest Hideaway

North side of Marigot Bay ☎451-4485 or 286-0511. Sun noon–10pm, Mon & Wed–Sat noon–3pm & 6–10pm. A subdued and glamorous atmosphere pervades this wood-panelled bar, where there is live jazz three or four times a week.

Soufrière and the Pitons

Picturesque Soufrière, St Lucia's largest west coast settlement, dwells in the shadows of the imposing Pitons. It offers easy access to the central forest reserves (see p.134) as well as many of the island's best historical and natural sights, such as cocoa and sugar plantations, waterfalls, botanical gardens and more. Local waters also hold some of St Lucia's most stunning reefs, enticing divers and snorkellers alike.

The southest coast is dominated by the majestic volcanic peaks of Petit Piton and Gros Piton, which rise out of the sea. Visible on a clear day from as far north as the hills of Castries, their breathtaking cones are undoubtedly St Lucia's most photographed feature.

Soufrière

Charming in its lack of polish, the quiet town of Soufrière is filled with a mix of architectural styles that includes everything from slapped-together wooden fishing huts to modern cement blocks. Soufrière is small enough to explore on foot, and the abundance of jammed, one-way streets and the lack of parking render vehicles inadvisable in any case.

A jumble of piers and boat slips where local fishing craft and tourist party boats dock, the waterfront is home to a small **fish market**, housed in a blue building behind the *Pirate's Cove Restaurant*. The nearby **fruit and vegetable market** is a more haphazard

▼ SOUFRIÈRE

Water taxis

Along the waterfront, you can catch convenient **water taxis** that traverse the area of Castries and around: boats service all of the nearby bays, many of which are difficult to access from the land without your own car (try Moby Dick Water Taxi ☏ 459-5651 or 484-6224). Costs per person are US$10 return trip to Anse Chastanet; US$30 return trip to Jalousie Beach; and US$30 round trip to Marigot Bay. Water taxis also offer sightseeing trips to Castries and back (US$350 for four people). One-way trips (no sightseeing) for four or more people start at US$90–100.

affair, with piles of produce sold right on the waterfront and the surrounding streets. A well-maintained walkway runs along the northern waterfront, where ornate streetlamps, benches and poinciana trees make for a pleasant evening stroll. The promenade ends near a small crafts centre (Mon–Sat 9am–4pm), which showcases local artisans selling carvings, straw hats and the like at reasonable prices. Next door, the office of the Soufrière Regional Development Foundation (☏459-7200) features displays on the local fishing industry and Soufrière Marine Park, which encompasses over 11km of coastline from Anse L'Ivrogne south of Gros Piton to Anse Jambon, just north of Anse Chastanet.

The grassy town square, enclosed by a low stone fence, sits a block inland from the waterfront. It was laid out by Soufrière's original French inhabitants in the eighteenth century and, notoriously, was the scene of numerous executions during the dark days of the Revolution. It's a peaceful and shady space today, bordered by businesses and homes built in the classic French colonial style, with second-floor balconies and intricate decorative woodwork. The J.Q. Charles dry goods store at the square's southwest corner is one of

the more ornate examples, with fretwork patterned after snowflakes. Dominating the east end of the square, the 1953 Lady of Assumption Church was built on the site of several older churches destroyed by earthquakes and fire – Soufrière has has the bad luck of being pummelled by hurricanes in 1780, 1817, 1831, 1898 and 1980 and rocked by an earthquake in 1839; in 1955, half the town was razed to the ground by a fire.

Soufrière is a pleasant place to stroll around, but you may experience some low-grade hassle from men who want to point your car in the right

▼ LADY OF ASSUMPTION CHURCH

PLACES Soufrière and the Pitons

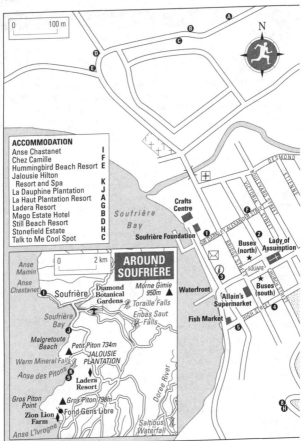

ACCOMMODATION

Anse Chastanet	I
Chez Camille	F
Hummingbird Beach Resort	E
Jalousie Hilton	
Resort and Spa	K
La Dauphine Plantation	J
La Haut Plantation Resort	A
Ladera Resort	G
Mago Estate Hotel	B
Still Beach Resort	D
Stonefield Estate	H
Talk to Me Cool Spot	C

AROUND SOUFRIÈRE

direction for cash or claim (falsely) to be collecting money for a charity. A firm "no" will usually be the end of it. The local police are aware of this activity and do their best to stop it.

Anse Chastanet

2km north of Soufrière. Popular Anse Chastanet is a long, wide beach that's presided over by a resort of the same name (see p.108). Because of a pristine reef that lies within swimming distance, Anse Chastanet offers some of St Lucia's best snorkelling,

and is a great starting point for scuba excursions, with several good dive sites nearby; Scuba St Lucia (www.scubastlucia.com), right on the beach, rents scuba equipment as well as snorkelling gear. The resort also has a great beach bar and restaurant, and while the beach chairs are for hotel guests, you're free to spread your towel on the sand.

Anse Mamin

Pretty, secluded Anse Mamin is accessible by water taxi or by a narrow footpath along the shore

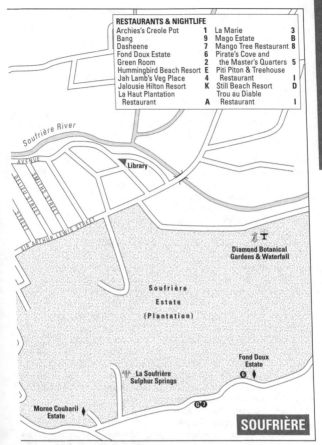

RESTAURANTS & NIGHTLIFE

Archies's Creole Pot	1	La Marie	3
Bang	9	Mago Estate	B
Dasheene	7	Mango Tree Restaurant	8
Fond Doux Estate	6	Pirate's Cove and	
Green Room	2	the Master's Quarters	5
Hummingbird Beach Resort	E	Piti Piton & Treehouse	
Jah Lamb's Veg Place	4	Restaurant	I
Jalousie Hilton Resort	K	Still Beach Resort	D
La Haut Plantation		Trou au Diable	
Restaurant	A	Restaurant	I

Soufrière River

Library

AVENUE

DELUGE STREET

SMITHS STREET

STREET

SIR ARTHUR LEWIS STREET

Diamond Botanical
Gardens & Waterfall

Soufrière
Estate
(Plantation)

La Soufrière
Sulphur Springs

Fond Doux
Estate

Morne Coubaril
Estate

SOUFRIÈRE

at low tide. A little-used scallop of tawny sand fronts the grounds of a former sugar plantation, where visitors can try jungle biking (⊛www.bikestlucia.com) through kilometres of hilly terrain and ruins.

Soufrière Estate and Diamond Botanical Gardens

About 2km east of Soufrière, along the inland road to the hamlet of Fond St Jacques ☎459-7565 or 459-7155. Mon–Sat 10am–5pm, Sun 10am–3pm. EC$7. A former

Visitors' information

Soufrière's **tourist office** (Mon–Fri 8am–4pm, Sat 8am–noon; ☎459-7419), on the waterfront and across from the main pier, is a handy source of local information; additionally, staff can direct you to members of the tourism department's helpful guide corps, who are uniformed in flowered shirts and give walking tours of the town.

eighteenth-century sugar plantation, Soufrière Estate was originally part of a 2000-acre land grant bestowed by Louis XIV to the prominent Deveaux family in 1713, and still in the family today. The estate is one of the oldest on the island, with a sugar mill built in 1765.

Most of the land is private today, but part of the former sugar plantation can be explored in the **Diamond Botanical Gardens** – well worth a visit, with mineral baths and a waterfall contained in lush grounds. The large, manicured gardens are networked by well-marked and easy-to-follow paths and packed with dozens of tropical species, including brilliant hibiscus in red, pink and white, yellow allamanda, sweet-smelling frangipani trees, the oddly shaped lobster claw and a number of different palms, as well as cocoa trees, tall Norfolk pines and elaborate casuarinas and flamboyants. There's also a Japanese water garden, on a side path that loops back to the main walkway, with small and ethereal arrangements of flowers and trees laid out in classic Japanese style. Brochures containing maps are available at the admission desk for an extra charge of EC$2.50.

The main path through the gardens follows the thin Diamond River to a sibilant ten-metre cascade fed by a mix of natural streams and underground thermal sulphur springs from the La Soufrière volcano. Splashing over rocks and shimmering with different colours caused by the sulphur content, the waterfall is aesthetic but unfortunately unsuitable for swimming due to pollution. Adjacent to the waterfall, thermal mineral baths are built on the site of the original facilities commissioned by Louis XVI in 1784. Reconstructed by Andre deBoulay in 1925, the springs are said to cure ailments such as rheumatism and arthritis; some people even drink the water, believing this to be a more direct route to curing internal ills. You can also splash about in the slightly pungent but warm depths of an outdoor pool or in several smaller tubs inside the bathhouse. In addition to the main entry fee to the complex, you'll pay EC$6.50 to use the pool and EC$10 for a private bath.

Toraille Falls

Daily 9am–5pm. EC$5. Gorgeous Toraille Falls, a 15-metre waterfall, is set in a tropical garden. You can sit in the pool beneath the cascade or on benches, or hike the upper trail behind the falls, where hummingbirds, ginger lilies and a stunning view of Petit Piton vie for attention. Come early in the morning or late in the afternoon to avoid the tour bus crowds.

▼ DIAMOND BOTANICAL GARDENS' WATERFALL

Morne Coubaril Estate

Less than 1km south of Soufrière on the road to Vieux Fort ☏459-7340, ⊛www.coubaril.com. Daily 9am–4.30pm. EC$20; with guided hike EC$40. Morne Coubaril is a 250-acre working plantation that also serves as a rather lacklustre tourist attraction. The plantation house, a private residence, is closed to visitors, but you can catch an informative thirty-minute walking tour (conducted by guides clad in eighteenth-century garb) that allows you to take in a small working sugar mill, recreations of slave huts and cocoa and cassava fields.

Perhaps what's most attractive about the estate are the two-hour guided hikes that start at nearby Sulphur Springs (see next), taking in the forest, waterfalls and thermal pools, and ending at the Morne Coubaril hill on the plantation grounds. Unfortunately, you will probably be one of a group of twenty or more as, generally, the tours are for cruiseship passengers or through Sunlink Tours (see p.148). Full-day and half-day horseback tours of the estate and the surrounding area are also available.

La Soufrière Sulphur Springs

South of Soufrière town, off the road to Vieux Fort. Daily 9am–5pm. EC$7.

Misleadingly billed as the world's only drive-in volcano, La Soufrière Sulphur Springs was a volcano measuring some 13km in diameter before it erupted and collapsed into itself around 40,000 years ago. La Soufrière remains active to this day – theoretically, it could erupt at any time – but as it is now classified as a solfatara, meaning it emits gases and vapours rather than lava and hot ash, a molten shower is extremely unlikely.

Turn into the springs at the signed road and you'll know you're in the midst of a volcano – killed off by sulphuric emissions, the vegetation becomes sparse and an eggy odour hangs in the air. After leaving your vehicle in the car park just metres from the most active part of the volcanic area, official (and very informative) guides will walk you up to the viewing platforms that overlook sections of the crater – seven barren acres of steaming, bubbling pools of sulphur-dense water and rocks tinged green and yellow. The pervasive acrid

▲ LA SOUFRIÈRE SULPHUR SPRINGS

Local legends

La Soufrière has long been a place of myth and superstition: old and dubious legends claim that Arawak Indians used the site for human sacrifice (despite the fact that there's little evidence of such activity in their culture), while the querulous but evidently cautious Caribs are thought to have called it *Qualibou*, meaning "a place of death".

smell is perhaps La Soufrière's most memorable aspect – something like rotting onions in an omelette gone bad.

Petit Piton

Beyond their aesthetic appeal, the Pitons offer an opportunity for high adventure. Petit Piton, according to the St Lucian government, stands at 734m and has been scaled in the past; though the climb is discouraged by local authorities – there are fragile ecosystems to take into account, as well as the inherent difficulty (and danger) of climbing a near-vertical slab of rock – some seem willing to clamber up nonetheless. The reward for such an effort is a bird's-eye view of the dramatically carved coastline and densely forested mountains of the interior. If you want to give it a try, you should be very fit and be sure to hire a guide

from town; ask at the Soufrière tourism office (see p.103) or at the Regional Development Foundation (☎459-7200).

Gros Piton

While more manageable than Petit Piton, hiking Gros Piton, which rises to 798m, is still a challenge. It's a long and hot ascent (bring sunscreen, plenty of water and something to eat), and you'll need to start out in the cool of early morning to ensure that you'll get back down before nightfall. Because the path branches off in several places, a guide is necessary. Depending on your level of fitness, the hike will take two to four hours round-trip. It starts out low and level along a rudimentary, rocky path and gently ascends until about 300m from the peak. After that, it's a steep, rocky climb – there are tree trunks and brush to hang

▼ PETIT & GROS PITON

Fond Gens Libre

Fond Gens Libre, a shady forest hamlet of about one hundred residents huddled at the base of Gros Piton, was the first settlement of runaway slaves and free blacks on St Lucia. When the British retook the island in 1796 and repealed the French revolutionary regime's abolition of slavery, hundreds of former slaves – known as brigands – refused to be resubjugated and took to the forest, from where they staged raids on plantations and other symbols of colonialism.

Flore Bois Galliard, the daughter of a French father and an African mother, ran this brigand hideout, and the caves where her band slept and cooked are still visible. Eventually she was captured and beheaded in Soufrière's town square, and today **Piton Flore** is named in her honour.

Gros Piton Tours (see p.156) has established an interesting interpretive centre in town, with exhibits on the flora, fauna and geology of the Pitons, and has begun to collect oral histories from Fond Gens Libre's older residents. Additionally, they offer guided hikes up Gros Piton and cultural and historical tours of the area. There is a simple restaurant and shop in the village, and traditional thatched huts to accommodate hikers are under construction.

Fond Gens Libre can be reached from the Gros Piton Trail access road signposted from the highway south of Soufrière, or on a more picturesque route from Choiseul (see p.118).

on to, and some rudimentary stone steps built to prevent erosion. The summit itself is a rocky, level area with marvellous views: on a clear day you'll see the neighbouring islands of St Vincent to the south and Martinique to the north, east over rolling farmland to Moule à Chique and up the mountainous interior all the way to Castries.

Anse L'Ivrogne

Visible from the southern slopes of Gros Piton, Anse L'Ivrogne is a little-visited expanse of golden sand, accessible by a half-hour hike on a spur trail from Gros Piton Trailhead at Fond Gens Libre, or by water taxi from Soufrière. Gros Piton Tours (see p.156) offers a combined guided hike, swim and barbeque on the beach.

Zion Lion Farm

At Anse L'Ivrogne. Call Paul Clifford (☎712-8907) or Nickey Jean Baptiste (☎712-1449) to arrange a visit. Situated along the sea at Anse L'Ivrogne, Zion Lion Farm is a Roots Culture (Rastafarian) farm and orchard offering an intriguing menu of cultural tours and activities, including Creole cooking classes; a guided walk through the organic gardens and surrounding forest; overnight camping with stargazing and traditional "konte" storytelling on New Moon nights (call ahead to reserve camping and breakfast); horseback trail rides; and much more. Kids up to 10 years old are admitted for free, and return transportation from area hotels is provided (for a fee) by a colourful wooden fishing pirogue.

Anse des Pitons

This blanket of soft white sand edges a gently curved cove separating the twin peaks of the Pitons and provides stunning views of both. It sits on the chichi *Jalousie Hilton* resort property (non-guests are admitted; see p.109) and is often well-populated, with a busy beachside restaurant and souvenir kiosks on-site. The beach is several shades lighter than most on the island because the gleaming white sand was imported from Guyana to satisfy the mostly upscale clientele. There's good snorkelling here, and equipment can be rented on the beach.

Warm Mineral Waterfalls
On the access road into the *Jalousie Hilton* from the highway. Daily 6.30am–7pm. EC$5. A picturesque and pleasantly tepid mix of spring water and thermal volcanic emissions, Warm Mineral Waterfalls pours down 30m into a natural heated pool, which makes for an energizing swim.

Malgretoute Beach
On the access road into the *Jalousie Hilton* from the highway. Formerly the site of a leper colony, today this strand of black sand backed by tall palms is a secluded spot for a picnic and a swim.

Zaka Masks
On the access road into the *Jalousie Hilton* from the highway ☎384-2925. The artisans at the Zaka Masks studio and shop create colourful, whimsical masks out of local woods.

Fond Doux Estate
Set back from the main Soufrière–Vieux Fort road, 3km from La Soufrière and just south of *Ladera Resort* ☎459-7545. Daily 9am–5pm. EC$20 including tour. This gorgeous, 250-year-old working cocoa estate sells its produce to local grocers in the form of cocoa sticks, and to Hershey's as the base for their famous chocolate. In the late eighteenth century, the estate was also the site of the Battle of Rabot, a bloody conflict between recently liberated St Lucian brigands and the British; musket balls have been found on the ground, and knowledgeable guides will show you these (as well as the extensive gardens and the plantation itself) on an informative walking tour.

The explanation of the cocoa-making process is a definite highlight, and visitors get to sample the raw, bitter pods straight from the tress, as well as visit the cocoa ovens used to dry them and the "cocoa dancing" shed, where men dance on the beans with their bare feet to polish them. There's an excellent Creole restaurant here (see p.112) and a glass of local juice or punch is included in the entrance fee.

Accommodation

Anse Chastanet Resort
Anse Chastanet ☎459-7000 or 1-800/223-1108 (US), ⊛www .ansechastanet.com. This spectacularly situated, smoothly run and supremely enjoyable holiday resort is built into a steep hillside along the beach. All of the 49 spacious guest suites are architecturally unique and decorated with original art, creating a luxurious atmosphere. While the balconied one-bedroom suites are a gorgeous blend of terracotta tile, natural woods, stone and fine fabrics, the panoramic view from Room 7F (the Royal Palm) requires you to make a reservation 9–10 months in advance. There are two wonderful restaurants (see p.114) and bars, and for those with the dosh, this is the ideal base for an active vacation. A great dive operator is on-site, and a multitude of spectacular

▲ HUMMINGBIRD BEACH RESORT

dive sites are close at hand; additionally, there is a jungle/mountain biking outfit and nearly 20km of trails; guided sea kayaking expeditions; highly recommended guided historical and nature hikes; and much more. The wide swath of soft brown sand in the sheltered cove is one of the nicest swimming beaches on the island. An even more glamorous set of open-sided clifftop suites, each with an in-room infinity pool, is set to open in late 2006 at $1000 a night. $495.

Chez Camille

Church St and Boulevard St, Soufrière ☎459-5379. *Camilla's* restaurant at 7 Bridge Street is the contact for these two downtown guesthouses, both called *Chez Camille* and separated by a couple of blocks. Basic but cosy rooms are equipped with fans and mosquito nets; most share cold-water bathrooms. Each location has a small common room with a TV, and guests get a ten percent discount in *Camilla's* restaurant. No credit cards. $85.

Hummingbird Beach Resort

Anse Chastanet Rd, Soufrière ☎459-7232 or 459-7985, ☜www.nvo.com/pitonresort. Some of the nine rooms at this small inn on the north edge of town are very attractive, with reproduction plantation-era furniture and private verandahs facing the nicely landscaped courtyard pool. The other rooms are rather worn, so try to have a look before you choose. All have overhead fans, mosquito nets and TV, and some have a/c; the standard (shared bath) rooms are attractively priced for budget travellers, but the rest are overpriced for what they offer. There is a small but swimmable patch of beach in front and a pleasant pool patio. The affiliated cottage across the road sleeps four. Rates include continental breakfast. Doubles $70, suite $170, cottage $285.

Jalousie Hilton Resort and Spa

Anse des Pitons, about 3km south of Soufrière. Reservations ☎456-8042 or 1-888/744-5256 (US); hotel ☎456-8000, ☜www.thejalousie plantation.com. Despite the absolutely stunning setting between the Pitons and efforts to make the chain's St Lucian venture feel like anything but a *Hilton*, this resort lacks the individuality and romantic charm of others in its price category. Even the mountain views, individual villas, powdery white-sand beach and luxury amenities (like private plunge pools, a spa and fitness facilities) don't give it much soul. The food is costly but good, if often far from local, and as no private cars are allowed to drive on the *Hilton's* hundreds of acres, guests must walk or rely on hotel shuttles and may find themselves compelled to stay on-site. Villas $480, suites $570.

Ladera Resort

Soufrière–Vieux Fort Rd ☎459-7323 or 800/738-4752 (US), ⊛www.ladera .com. Exquisite views of the sea framed by the twin peaks of the Pitons, inspired architectural design and a friendly and professional staff make this intimate and exclusive hilltop resort the epitome of luxurious relaxation. All 25 villas and suites are open on one side, and the soothing, richly polished wood interiors, open-air cliffside showers and private plunge pools may mean you never leave your room. If you do, there is also an inviting pool deck, a relaxed bar and reading lounge, a spa and an excellent restaurant. Given the hilltop location, there is no beach and no grounds to speak of, but there are shuttles to nearby beaches and other diversions are easily arranged. Suites $450, villa $590.

Le Haut Plantation Resort

About 2.5 km north of Soufrière on the West Coast Rd ☎459-7008, ⊛www .lahaut.com. Set high in the hills above Soufrière with a spectacular and sweeping view of the whole Soufrière valley, this small guesthouse, on a working 52-acre plantation, is a tranquil retreat. The half-dozen rooms are spacious and airy, comfortably furnished and equipped with full kitchens. Each has a patio or verandah, and there's a a cosy lounge with a library, pool table and TV. In addition to the rooms, a three-bedroom/three-bathroom villa with its own pool is available. The reasonably priced restaurant (see p.113) serves delicious local food, while the poolside bar is perfect for a sunset drink. An excellent continental breakfast is included in the rates. Doubles $175, cottage $225.

Mago Estate Hotel

Soufrière–Castries Rd ☎459-7352 or 459-5880, ⊛www .magohotel.com. Perched on a steep hillside, this small, boutique hotel has a lovely view of the mountains and Soufrière harbour. Ten unique rooms have mahogany four-poster beds, stone floors strewn with oriental carpets and wide jalousied windows framing the scenery. The nicest are the stone and wood "Shangri-La" rooms, with sumptuous furnishings and rough-hewn elegance, open on one side to the view. "Eco-value" rooms (which are cooled by fans rather than a/c) are

▲ VIEW FROM LADERA RESORT

similar in style, but a bit cramped and therefore relatively less expensive, and the air-conditioned "Eden" suites have private plunge pools, a kitchenette and TV. Yoga, Qi Gong and massages are on offer, plus there's a freshwater pool rimmed with stones. A wonderfully atmospheric treehouse lounge is built around the trunk of a massive mango tree, and a very romantic restaurant is nestled at the top (see p.114). Rates include continental breakfast. Doubles $175, suites $325.

Still Beach Resort

Anse Chastanet Rd ☎459-5179 or 459-7261, ⊛www.thestillresort.com. Spacious, clean and balconied doubles and one-bedroom apartments overlook the beach on the edge of town, affording lovely views of Soufrière Bay and Petit Piton. The beach is not one of the island's best, but it's nice enough for a stroll or quick dip, and the dive shop offers lower rates than its competitors. The restaurant serves good Creole food (see p.115). Doubles $120, apartments $145.

Stonefield Estate

Soufrière–Vieux Fort Rd, about 2km south of Soufrière ☎459-5648 or 459-7037, ⊛www.stonefieldvillas.com. These fifteen spacious and secluded villas are scattered over the well-tended slopes of an old plantation and tucked in amongst mango and banana trees. Each airy and tastefully appointed villa has a full kitchen, a large sitting/dining area, and bedrooms with wide jalousied windows and open-air showers fringed with flowering plants. A pool, restaurant (see p.114) and bar are situated to maximize the mountain views,

and there is a free shuttle to take you to the beach. One-bedroom villas $225.

Talk to Me Cool Spot

West Coast Rd, Soufrière ☎459-7437, ⊛www.talk-2me.com. Visitors at this inexpensive guesthouse are made to feel like family, especially when eating the tasty home-made Caribbean cooking in the restaurant. Studio rooms are small and rustic (curtained in-room toilets and showers), but doubles are spacious and decorated with hand-painted murals. Unique views of Petit Piton and Soufrière make up for noises wafting up the hill from town. $75.

Restaurants

Archie's Creole Pot

9 Bridge St, Soufrière ☎459-7760/5771. Daily 8am–til late. Popular with locals and visitors alike, this cheerful restaurant and bar specializes in skilfully prepared local Creole cuisine (including vegetarian options) and Indian dishes. A great choice for a casual, inexpensive meal.

Bang

Anse des Pitons ☎459-7864. Daily noon–midnight. An eccentric British aristocrat has transported a collection of wooden colonial-era buildings from Castries and resurrected them waterside – bang between the Pitons. One cottage houses a simple, moderately priced lunch counter and ice-cream shop, and an inviting open-air restaurant serves spicy, Jamaican jerk-style barbecued fish, chicken and other meats. On Wednesdays a floorshow features music, fire-eaters, limbo dancers and acrobats.

Dasheene

In *Ladera Resort*, Soufrière-Vieux Fort Rd ☎459-7323. Daily 7–10am, noon–2.30pm & 6.30pm–9pm. An artful and eclectic mix of West Indian, Asian and Italian cuisines is served here. Dasheen and coconut cappuccino soup is topped with fresh nutmeg; a trio of island meats (curried lamb, cajun chicken and jerk pork) is offered atop black-eyed bean risotto with a ginger jus; and vegetarians may wish to try the pumpkin and christophene tart with a spinach cheese sauce. Dinner is usually excellent, but the buffets can be mediocre and lunch is hit-or-miss. The all-afternoon pool/bar menu offers simpler and less expensive options, including rotis, sandwiches and burgers and fresh fish or chicken rolled in banana crumbs, then deep-fried and served with calypso sauce. The cosy natural wood setting and the view of the Pitons and bay below are also inviting – stop by for a drink before sunset.

Fond Doux Estate

Soufrière-Vieux Fort Rd. Open daily Nov–April 9am–4pm and for lunch Tues, Fri; Sat in low season. The excellent, moderately priced buffet lunch (EC$25) offered here includes fish, chicken and tasty vegetable dishes, as well as fruit juices made with fresh produce grown on-site. Tables are on covered wooden patios surrounded by fruit trees and coconut palms.

Green Room

Church St, Soufrière ☎457-1324. Daily 9am–11pm. At this informal neighbourhood restaurant, dishes (EC$20–45) include creole or grilled tuna, chicken or stewed lamb neck with large sides of local fruits and vegetables like dasheen, plantain and breadfruit.

Hummingbird Beach Resort

Anse Chastanet Rd, Soufrière ☎459-7232. This popular tourist hangout is especially favoured for drinks at sunset on the beachside pool patio; additional seating is available at cosy, richly upholstered banquettes in a romantic whitewashed stone-and-dark-wood dining alcove. There are fresh juices, pastries, eggs and French toast for breakfast; salads, baguette sandwiches and fish and burgers for lunch; and dinner includes seafood such as conch, king crab and octopus. The service is exasperatingly slow, though if you're eating at the restaurant you'll have access to the hotel's small pool, beach and showers.

Jah Lamb's Veg Place

5 High St, Soufrière. Daily 11.30am–3.30pm. Locally famous for its tasty vegetarian fare, this friendly eatery caters primarily to the Rastafarian community, with practically free fresh-

▲ FOND DOUX ESTATE

▲ JAH LAMB'S VEG PLACE

baked pizza (EC$5), vegetable burgers (EC$3), dhal (lentil stew, EC$2) and boullion (soup EC$9). There are a few tables in the front room and takeaway is available.

Jalousie Hilton Resort

Anse des Pitons ☎ 459-7666. There are three pricey but decent restaurants within this glitzy resort (see p.109). In the Great House, the refined *Plantation* serves international cuisine (make reservations and dress up a bit), while on the water, at the south end of the property, the *Pier* is a more informal dinner option. On the beach, the perennially crowded *Bayside* serves lighter meals for breakfast and lunch, as well as a dinner buffet that features live entertainment

Le Haut Plantation Restaurant

In *Le Haut Plantation Resort*, Castries–Soufrière Rd ☎ 459-7008. Closed Mon. This very reasonably priced restaurant serves excellent, fresh local fare – and lots of it – in a truly breathtaking hillside setting overlooking

the Pitons and the sweeping bowl of hills and mountains sourrounding Soufrière. Appetizers include pumpkin or callaloo soup, seafood, chicken or spinach crepes or fishcakes (around EC$18); mains feature curried beef or coconut chicken, breaded flying fish and vegetable dishes (around EC$36).

La Marie

16 Bay St, Soufrière ☎ 459-5002. Daily 9am–11pm; June–Oct noon–11pm. At this bright second-floor restaurant, large windows offer a panoramic view of the harbour and cheerful, hand-painted Zaka masks decorate the walls. The moderately priced, expertly prepared cuisine is Caribbean with a twist – meals include seafood chowder with cognac and crusty French-bread sandwiches filled with flying fish, spicy jerk chicken or brie and spring onion. There are also steak, seafood and chicken dinners and, although billed as a "light meal", the rotis are filling, delicious and a great buy at EC$12–15.

Mago Estate

West Coast Hwy, just north of Soufrière, ☏459-5880. Daily. Carved out of the hillside above Soufrière, this romantic dining room has low benches built into the sloping exposed rock walls, trees growing up through the floors and ceilings and North African furnishings evocative of a candlelit stone palace. In contrast, the menu is a mix of French Creole cooking and European cuisine. Appetizers like wild spinach and christophene soup sprinkled with crusted black peppercorn and garlic run US$8–15; mains, which may include stir-fried pork and green mango in a black bean and sherry sauce are from US$22 to $27.

Mango Tree Restaurant

In *Stonefield Estate*, Soufrière–Vieux Fort Rd ☏459-7586. Daily 7.30am–10pm. One of St Lucia's most enjoyable dining experiences, the delicious, locally inspired menu at this hillside restaurant features everything from fresh pumpkin soup to jerk chicken and vegetarian pasta for lunch; freshly baked chocolate and banana cakes for afternoon tea (or breakfast); and seasonal vegetables with the fresh catch-of-the-day from Soufrière's fish market for dinner. Lunch costs around EC$25, and dinner averages EC$30-40.

Pirate's Cove and the Master's Quarters

Soufrière waterfront ☏459-5002, ⓦwww.piratescovestlucia.com. Daily 8am–midnight. This handsome waterfront building, which houses two restaurants, dates from 1898 – its bathrooms were once courthouse cells. The cuisine is a fusion of West Indian and Southeast Asian styles and, despite its average, overpriced food and some management kinks, reservations are essential for both places in high season. The more casual *Pirate's Cove* restaurant, pleasantly situated on the verandah, serves burgers, rotis, pasta and seafood dishes for EC$20–50; formal dining and a more elaborate menu is found in the *Master's Quarters* upstairs, where mains range from EC$36 to EC$75.

Piti Piton and Treehouse Restaurant

In *Anse Chastanet Resort* ☏459-7000. Daily for breakfast (8–10:30am) and afternoon tea (3:30–5:30pm); dinner daily 6–10pm except Tues and Fri. Bar none, this is the finest

▼ MAGO ESTATE

gourmet dining experience on the island. The setting, at the *Anse Chastanet Resort* (see p.108), is sunny and inviting by day and romantic and candlelit by night; the views take in the surf below and across the bay to Petit Piton. Incorporating fresh local produce and seafood, the exquisite dinner menu changes daily and may include offerings such as delicately spicy Caribbean gazpacho served with fresh crusty Creole bread; plaintain and goat cheese fritters; and a chocolate and roasted coconut terrine that will bring chocolate lovers to their knees. The breakfast buffet features lots of fresh fruit, hot dishes and pastries, and there are water pistols on your table to shoo away the chattering, thieving songbirds. Dinner plus wine is a well-spent EC$40–80.

Still Beach Resort

Anse Chastanet Rd ☎459-5179 or 459-7261. Daily 7.30am–11pm. Mostly Creole-based and spicy, the menu here include saltfish, green figs and omelettes for breakfast, while lunch and dinner (mains are around EC$25) usually consist of pepperpot soup, sweet-and-sour flying fish or freshwater prawns. The restaurant is set on the beach under an ocean-facing canopy and has a lovely, seaside view of the Pitons.

Trou au Diable Restaurant

In *Anse Chastanet Resort* ☎459-7000. Open daily for lunch and Mon–Sat 6:30–9:30pm for a dinner buffet. The extensive menu at this torch-lit, beachside restaurant features creative dishes such as cajun grilled chicken with Piton beer barbeque sauce;

deep-fried squid with a tomato chili dip; and the fish of the day baked with tomato, marjoram, cinnamon and red wine. You can also choose from pasta, baguette sandwiches, rotis and burgers, plus cheese melts served with green papaya coleslaw and plantain chips or fried sweet potatoes with honey and mustard (US$7–10). While the food can be just okay, the service and atmosphere are excellent. Reservations are required for dinner. The attached bar serves an array of luscious frosty cocktails.

Bars and clubs

Anse Chastanet Resort

Anse Chastanet ☎459-7000 or 1-800/223-1108 (US), ⊛www .ansechastanet.com. *Anse Chastanet Resort's* casually elegant *Piton Bar* has live music every night – St Lucian folk, jazz or soft piano music – to accompany dinner. The comfy waterside lounging chairs at the more casual *Trou au Diable Bar* on the beach is a wonderful spot for a sundowner and conversation.

Archie's Bar

9 Bridge St, Soufrière ☎459-7760. This is the place to rub shoulders with the locals, catch the drift of current events and maybe play a game of dominoes.

Dasheene

Ladera Resort, Soufrière-Vieux Fort Rd ☎459-7323, ⊛www.ladera.com. For a spectacular and memorable sunset cocktail, park yourself ringside on a bar stool in the treehouse-like bar at the *Ladera Resort*.

The south coast

A world away from the tourism hub in the island's north-west region, St Lucia's rural south coast boasts some striking, pastoral scenery. The narrow mountain highway whirls and dips inland before swinging towards the ocean, through the peaceful fishing villages of Choiseul and Laborie, past hillside farms and across several rivers, finally descending onto the broad coastal plain surrounding Vieux Fort.

Despite the fact that nearly all foreign visitors arrive at Vieux Fort's Hewanorra International Airport, large resorts are almost non-existent in this part of the island. The area does, however, have its share of natural attractions and historical sites, including the Balenbouche Estate, with its lovingly preserved plantation home and eighteenth-century sugar mill; the Saturday morning country market in Laborie's village square; a scenic riverbank hiking trail to the Saltibus waterfall; spectacular island-wide views from Cap Moule à Chique; and a long ribbon of lightly used white sand at Anse de Sables, facing the Maria Islands Nature Reserve, which lies a short distance offshore.

Choiseul

Quiet Choiseul is a compact village with little to see or do save exploring the waterfront, with its weathered stone Catholic church and busy fishing sheds. The wide, dark-sand Choiseul Community Beach, just a two-minute drive north of the waterfront, has plenty of shade under the trees and lots of space for the volleyball court that's a favourite haunt amongst the village's youth.

▼ CHOISEUL

Choiseul Arts and Crafts Development Centre

On the main hwy at La Fargue. The small satellite settlement of La Fargue, east of Choiseul, is best known for the Choiseul Arts and Craft Development Centre (Mon–Sat; ☎459-3226). This is the best place on the south coast to buy locally produced crafts – prices are better than those at the tourist shops of

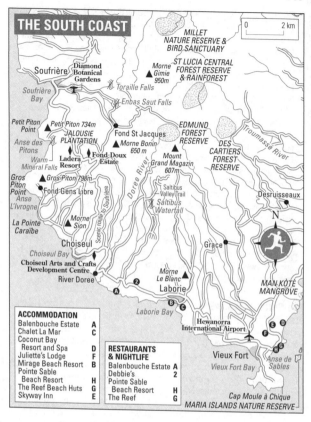

THE SOUTH COAST

0   2 km

MILLET
NATURE RESERVE &
BIRD SANCTUARY

Soufrière
Diamond
Botanical
Gardens

Morne
Gimie
950m

ST LUCIA CENTRAL
FOREST RESERVE
& RAINFOREST

Soufrière
Bay

Toraille Falls

Enbas Saut Falls

Petit Piton
Point

Petit Piton 734m
JALOUSIE
PLANTATION

Fond St Jacques

EDMUND
FOREST
RESERVE

Troumassé River

Anse des
Pitons

Morne Bonin
650 m

DES
CARTIERS
FOREST
RESERVE

Warm
Mineral Falls

Ladera
Resort

Fond-Doux
Estate

Mount
Grand Magazin
607m

Gros
Piton
Point

Gros Piton 798m

Fond Gens Libre

Saltibus
Valley Trail

Desruisseaux

Saltibus
Waterfall

Anse
L'Ivrogne

La Pointe
Caraïbe

Morne
Sion

Grace

N

Choiseul

Choiseul Bay

MAN KÔTÉ
MANGROVE

Choiseul Arts and Crafts
Development Centre

River Doree

Morne
Le Blanc

2

Laborie

A   B   C

Laborie Bay

B   C

ACCOMMODATION
Balenbouche Estate	A
Chalet La Mar	C
Coconut Bay	
Resort and Spa	D
Juliette's Lodge	F
Mirage Beach Resort	B
Pointe Sable	
Beach Resort	H
The Reef Beach Huts	G
Skyway Inn	E

Hewanorra
International Airport

E   D
F

**RESTAURANTS
& NIGHTLIFE**
Balenbouche Estate	A
Debbie's	2
Pointe Sable	
Beach Resort	H
The Reef	G

Vieux Fort

Vieux Fort Bay

Anse de
Sables

Cap Moule à Chique

MARIA ISLANDS NATURE RESERVE

larger towns. Artisans display their pottery, mats, carvings, wicker baskets and traditional wood furniture in the main building.

River Doree and the scenic backroad to Soufrière

The tidy roadside community of River Doree is home to the island's oldest church – a pretty little stone facade, built in 1901 – and you can also pick up a scenic backroad to Soufrière nearby. Just north of the village, the well-paved road heads inland at a junction at the top of the hill. It climbs up into the hills and along a ridge, through banana plantations and past tidy cottages and farms, with beautiful views of lush green ridges and valleys, emerging onto the main highway near a bridge at Victoria Junction, by a plant nursery. If you take the next inland turn-off on your right (if you are heading north) just a few hundred metres along, you can drive another (not quite so picturesque) backroad to the hillside community of Fond St Jacques, past the Touraille Falls (see p.104), and on into Soufrière.

Getting to La Pointe Caribe and Fond Gens Libre

Choiseul is bordered to the north by the small, scattered settlement of **La Pointe Caribe**, which was home to the last of St Lucia's Caribs until the nineteenth century. A few of their descendents still live here, some in thatched huts reminiscent of traditional Amerindian dwellings, and a few local artisans continue traditional clay pot making and basketry. If you'd like to visit and learn more about the local culture, contact Gros Piton Tours (see p.156).

The road from Choiseul to La Pointe Caribe (and on to **Fond Gens Libre** and the trailhead for Gros Pitons; see p.107) is very rough in parts, but driveable in a regular car and very scenic, passing old stone silo sugar mills on the velvety green ridges of Morne Sion, and across a couple of streams, with glimpses of the sea.

To reach La Pointe Caribe and Fond Gens Libre from the main street of Choiseul village (facing Soufrière), follow the road north to the edge of the settlement, then up a hill, down another hill, across a bridge, and up yet another hill to a T-junction, where there is a bus stop. Turn left and drive until you reach another junction with a bus shelter; turn left again and go straight until you reach a third bus shelter. Here, turn right and go up a hill, where you will see a sign to Gros Piton Nature Trail. Take this turn-off, and you will come to La Pointe Caribe and Dulcer village, passing the Delta school on the right and then the Dulcer Health Centre on the left. The turn-off for Fond Gens Libre and Gros Piton is signposted on the left as you leave the village. The drive from Choiseul to Fond Gens Libre takes about half an hour and offers an interesting glimpse into rural St Lucian life.

The Saltibus waterfall and trail

Further south along the Soufrière–Vieux Fort Rd you'll come across the Saltibus waterfall and trail, reached via the last turn-off on the main road before the well-signposted Balenbouche Estate. The trail is a strenuous but rewarding hour-and-a-quarter hike through the forest along the banks of the Saltibus River, bringing you to a lush and secluded spot where the cold mountain stream tumbles over a heap of boulders, leaving cool, inviting dipping pools at their base. The trail can be a bit difficult to locate on your own; if you would like to go with a guide, contact Gerald Butt (☎455-1239), who heads the local community group that maintains the trail.

Balenbouche Estate

Around 3km south of Choiseul ☎455-1244, ⓦwww.balenbouche .com. Daily 9am–5pm. EC$5; guided tours EC$15 (available on request, but advance notice is appreciated). Set on seventy acres, the verdant Balenbouche Estate surrounds a charming nineteenth-century plantation house with a peaked roof and wraparound porch. The white clapboard home is both a private family residence and a guesthouse (see p.123). About one third of the grounds are farmed (crops are sold at local markets), and much of the property is shaded by massive calabash, flamboyant, mango, breadfruit and banyan trees. Also on site are a picturesque, defunct water wheel and the remains of an old sugar mill dating from 1765, embedded in the mossy ground and surrounded by serpentine tree trunks.

The estate stretches down to the ocean, and a short walk toward the coast takes you to the Balenbouche River, which cuts through the property and is a lovely spot for quiet meditation. Along the shore are several soccer ball-sized rocks, which have smoothed basins hollowed into their tops and are believed to have been used by Arawaks as washing stones. The various petroglyph sites inland along the river further attest to a strong Amerindian presence in the area.

The best way to explore Balenbouche is to join one of the relaxed, informal walking tours (normally conducted by the owner or her equally-knowledgeable daughter). Good, healthy, home-made meals are served on the verandah with advance reservation (see p.125).

Laborie

Tiny Laborie, skirted by the west coast road, has a pretty turquoise bay sprinkled with brightly painted fishing boats and a few sandy lanes lined with wooden cottages. The shady village square hosts a lively Saturday morning market, and there is a nice stretch of palm-shaded public beach with good swimming on the western edge of town. Local entrepreneur Phillip Simeon

operates a seamoss farm on the waterfront and is always happy to let visitors sample his seamoss drink – an acquired taste which is supposed to be very good for your health.

While you lie on the beach looking up through palm fronds, you might muse on the fact that a coconut tree takes seven to ten years before it begins to bear fruit, and remains fertile for 70-80 years, producing 100 nuts a year. Be aware that, graceful and lovely as they are, coconut palms can be dangerous – the dark, ripe nuts can fall on your head with enough force to seriously hurt a person.

Le Blanc Nature Heritage viewpoint

On the inland side of the road just north of the Laborie turnoff, a sign points up a steep and rocky hill to the Le Blanc Nature Heritage viewpoint. Driving up the potholed road to the top of Morne Le Blanc is an act of faith, but the reward for the ten-minute journey is expansive views of Vieux Fort and the southeast and west coasts. There are two

PLACES The south coast

▼ LABORIE

▲ VIEUX FORT

viewing platforms here, but be careful when climbing them, as they appear not to have been attended to for some years.

Vieux Fort

Jammed with traffic and produce vendors, Vieux Fort, St Lucia's second largest town and its most southerly settlement, is a busy commercial centre and the base for businesses that service sprawling Hewanorra International Airport, just north of Downtown. Both the town and the airport lie on a relatively flat plain that slopes gently towards the north and the south-central mountains.

The best place to savour Vieux Fort's urban bustle is its main drag, Clarke Street, lined with shops, vendors and homes embellished with gingerbread fretwork in the classic Colonial style. A small, grassy square along Clarke Street has a bandstand, which serves as an occasional venue for St Lucia Jazz Festival performances (see p.157), while the west side of Downtown is bordered by a small wharf where fishing boats pull up on shore. Overall, however, there's little to do or see in the town centre.

Cap Moule à Chique

At the southern edge of Vieux Fort, the large and hilly promontory of Cap Moule à Chique juts into the sea and rises above the industrial port on Vieux Fort Bay – an inlet with storage warehouses and massive docks for large cargo ships. The lighthouse here was originally meant for Cape Saint Lucia, South Africa, but got shipped to the Caribbean by mistake.

A brief history of Vieux Fort

Until the early seventeenth century, the area around **Vieux Fort** was inhabited by the Arawaks, who are thought to have grown crops in the fertile plains that spread out beneath the interior mountains. Vieux Fort then came into prominence as a replenishing point for Dutch shippers, who built a small fort east of town on a promontory now called Pointe Sable to protect their supplies from the Caribs, thus giving the town its name – "Old Fort" in French. European dominion saw the arrival of large-scale cultivation – relatively flat land, an abundance of fresh water and soil rich from volcanic activity made the region suitable for growing sugar cane, and by the mid-eighteenth century, there were more than sixty estates in the area. The great plantations lasted until the 1920s, when sugarcane prices plummeted in the face of the cheaper and more easily produced beet sugar from other countries. Prosperity came to the area again during World War II, when Allied forces leased one thousand acres of land around Vieux Fort and built a military base and an airstrip, which was later enlarged to become Hewanorra International Airport.

On a clear day, the view from here is absolutely spectacular, with the long sweep of white sand on Anse de Sables and the green dots of the Maria Islands at its base; the incongruous cones of the Pitons to the west; a long view up the mountainous spine of the island to Pointe Hardy; and a glimpse of St Vincent on the southern horizon.

It can be tricky getting to Cap Moule à Chique, but begin by heading west on the main highway into Vieux Fort from the airport and turn left onto New Dock Rd at the roundabout as you enter town. Next go straight until you reach a "Y" junction in front of the Vieux Fort Secondary School. Take the left-hand fork and bear left again at the next junction (the other road drops down to the port). The road is a bit bumpy at first but soon becomes smooth, freshly paved tarmac, switchbacking up the steep peninsula, past the gate to the lighthouse to a small parking lot by the radio tower.

Anse de Sables

Stretching some 2km northward from the cliffs of Cap Moule

▼ CAP MOULE À CHIQUE

à Chique to Pointe Sable, the golden Anse de Sables beach is the only real option (and a fine one at that) for swimming near Vieux Fort. The clean, expansive seashore is free from the overcrowding and noise of some of the beaches in the north of the island and, thanks to mild surf, good breezes and Tornado – a windsurfing and kitesurfing operator at its southern end (Oct–June 9am–5pm; ☎454-7579, ⓦwww.tornado-surf .com) – it's a favoured spot for windsurfers. Cold drinks and casual meals (as well as rest rooms) are available at the *Pointe Sable Beach Resort* (see p.126), and the *Reef* bar next door (see p.126) rents beach chairs (EC$5 for the day).

Maria Islands Interpretive Centre

At the south end of Anse de Sables ☎454-5014. Mon–Fri 9am–4.30pm. In the shadow of the looming Cap Moule à Chique, the Maria Islands Interpretive Centre is a small natural history complex as well as the place to arrange a trip to the nearby Maria Islands (see next). The one-room museum (free) provides insight into the area's ecosystems and history, with displays on Amerindian culture (including a skull and other skeletal remains), mangroves and marine life; the fishing industry section has an example of a traditional dugout canoe called a *gonmyé*.

Maria Islands Nature Reserve

About 1km off the Anse de Sables shore ☎454-5014. Daily Sept–April. EC$94 for one person or EC$80.40 per person for groups of two or more. Two scrubby, windswept cays comprise the Maria Islands Nature Reserve. Both the hilly, 24-acre Maria Major and its sister islet, 4-acre Maria Minor, are breeding grounds for numerous sea birds, including the booby and frigate, and home to two species of reptiles, one of which – the kouwés snake (also spelled "couresse") – is found nowhere else in the world. The male *zandoli tè*, or ground lizard, which is around 35cm long and has a bright blue tail and a yellow belly, is also found only on the Maria Islands and nearby Praslin Island on the east coast (where some of their number where transferred due to the extreme aridity of the

▲ ANSE DE SABLES

▲ MARIA ISLANDS NATURE RESERVE

Marias in the dry season). The less ostentatious female is brown with darker vertical stripes.

Maria Major has a short but comely beach of golden sand, with a reef a few metres offshore that makes this a good spot for swimming and snorkelling. Several unmarked and unchallenging trails loop around the islands, taking you past sparse, cactus-strewn vegetation and rocky shoreline.

If you want to visit the Marias, you'll need to contact the Maria Islands Interpretive Centre. This is the only place where you can arrange a day-trip conducted by official St Lucia National Trust guides. The trips begin at the centre and consist of walking tours of the islands and stops for swimming and snorkelling (bring your own gear). Though you can arrange Saturday or Sunday trips, the centre is open only on weekdays, and its hours can be erratic – it's always best to call ahead. Note that the islands are closed to visitors between May and August, when several species of birds are nesting.

Accommodation

Balenbouche Estate

Balenbouche, near Piaye ☎455-1244, ⊛www.balenbouche.com. Lush grounds scattered with fruit trees and exotic flowers, picturesque ruins of a sugar mill and even a few Amerindian rock carvings are found on this charming, slightly dilapidated seventy-acre plantation just south of Choiseul. Rooms in the early nineteenth-entury estate house are clean, cosy (shared bath) and furnished with antiques; the imaginatively designed one- and two-bedroom cottages nestled in the trees nearby feature sofa swings, open-roofed showers and outdoor (covered) kitchens. Wonderful meals, served on the flower bedecked verandah, are

The kouwés snake

About a metre long with dark green and brown markings, the harmless **kouwés snake** once thrived on St Lucia's mainland, but was eradicated by the mongooses introduced by sugarcane planters to kill off troublesome rats, mice and other snakes. Today kouwés live only on Maria Major island and number a mere one hundred or so.

▲ BALENBOUCHE ESTATE

available on request, and a string of secluded beaches (small, but suitable for a quick dip and a lazy afternoon lolling on the sand) are just a short walk away. Doubles $80, cottages $180.

Chalet La Mar

Laborie ☎455-9194, ⊛www.slucia .com/lamar. There's only one charming little cottage here, furnished simply with two twin beds and featuring a kitchenette and a shady balcony with a lovely view of Laborie Bay. The village beach is a five-minute walk away. $50.

Coconut Bay Resort and Spa

Vieux Fort ☎758/456-9999, ⊛www .coconutbayresortandspa.com. A sprawling, 85-acre all-inclusive that sits on the beach, *Coconut Bay* is the only resort of its kind in the south. Though less than ten minutes from the airport, it's nonetheless quite isolated. Three pools, a waterpark and an activities centre will keep the kids happy, while tennis courts, a spa and jogging trails appeal to adults. $520.

Juliette's Lodge

Vieux Fort ☎454-5300, ⊛www .julietteslodge.com. Conveniently close to Hewanorra International Airport and Anse de Sables beach, *Juliette's* is popular amongst both airline crews and the windsurfer

crowd. The 24 rooms and three apartments are comfortable and clean, with a/c, cable TV and balconies affording views of the Maria Islands. There are mountain bikes for hire, plus there's a small pool and a lively restaurant serving basic but hearty fare. Doubles $100, studio apartment $130.

Kimatrai Hotel

Vieux Fort ☎454-6328, ⊛www .kimatraihotel.com. Though not a vacation resort, rooms here are bright and airy and include cable TV, mini-fridges and a/c; studios and apartments come with kitchens and overlook Vieux Fort's fishing port and the Caribbean Sea. There is a restaurant and bar on-site, and rates include continental breakfast. Doubles $55, studio apartments $65.

La Dauphine Plantation

Etangs, 7km south of Soufrière ☎450-2884, ⊛www.villabeachcottages .com. Set a short distance from the main road on the grounds of an old plantation, this is an economical choice for families or groups with a car, but perhaps too isolated for those relying on public transportation. Guests can choose from two-bedroom cottages and rooms in the restored nineteenth-century Great House. Doubles $155, cottages $120.

Mirage Beach Resort

Laborie Bay, Laborie ☎455-9763, ⊛www.cavip.com/mirage. Right on the water, this lovely spot offers five comfortable beachside rooms, all with kitchenettes and terraces. You can also opt to rent an apartment (sleeping two to four people) in the beach house. A pristine reef not far from shore makes for excellent snorkelling, plus there is a relaxing, open-air French/Creole restaurant and bar on-site. Doubles $75, apartments $95.

Pointe Sable Beach Resort

Anse de Sables, near Vieux Fort ☎454-6002, ©mjnbaptiste@hotmail.com. Four simple but decent beachfront guestrooms have balconies or patios, plus there's a restaurant and bar. $65.

The Reef Beach Huts

Anse de Sables ☎758/454-3418, ⓦwww.slucia.com/reef. A mostly windsurfer clientele is drawn to the four basic but attractive wood-panelled rooms here. There's no ocean view, but it's only a few steps from the beach. $50.

Skyway Inn

Beanfield, Vieux Fort ☎454-7111, ⓦwww.slucia.com/skyway. Large, comfortable rooms and a few studios are found at this basic airport hotel. A pool, a popular local bar and a restaurant serving good breakfasts are all on-site. The beach is a couple of minutes away. $75.

Restaurants

Balenbouche Estate

Balenbouche, near Piaye ☎455-1244. Open for lunch and dinner by reservation only. Cocktails from about 6pm with dinner served around 7pm. Dining on the verandah of this restored early nineteenth-century plantation house is a memorable experience. The gentle and gracious hostesses prepare a flavourful, wholesome and beautifully presented meal using fresh local produce, drawing on a repertoire of Creole and international recipes. The setting is delightful, with a sundappled view of the flower-beds by day and candlelight by night, with a serenade of tree frogs and soft music. A three-course dinner costs US$15 for hotel guests and US$20 for non-guests. The menu changes daily, but everyone is served the same meal.

Debbie's

Soufrière-Vieux Fort Rd, near Piaye ☎758/455-1625. Closed Sun. Mouthwatering feasts here include seafood, lamb, pork, chicken and vegetable dishes, with large portions of creamed pumpkin, mashed potatoes, fried plantains, corn cakes and breadfruit balls. Leave room for the home-made dessert, which may include anything from profiteroles to passionfruit cake. The covered terrace, where you dine, is lit with fairy lights at night.

The Old Plantation Yard

Commercial St, near the corner of Giraudy St, Vieux Fort ☎454-7969. Mon–Sat 7am–5pm; reservations essential for dinner. Wonderful dishes featuring local ingredients are prepared in a wooden cottage dating from 1890 and served at picnic tables on a shaded backyard patio. Stewed meats and fish broths are the specialities, but you should also try the selection of local juices and vegetable dishes. Come for a traditional Creole breakfast of roast bakes (bread), cocoa tea, saltfish and smoked herring on Saturday mornings. Live music is performed occasionally.

▲ THE OLD PLANTATION YARD

Pointe Sable Beach Resort

Anse de Sables, near Vieux Fort
☎454-6002. Daily breakfast, lunch,
dinner and evening drinks. A roomy
and colourful beachfront bar
and restaurant, serving burgers,
sandwiches and local dishes.
A meal runs EC$15–25.

The Reef

Anse de Sables ☎454-3418. Tues–Sun
8am–10pm; Mon high season
8am–6pm. This busy beachside
restaurant and bar has seating
outside under the trees and
Internet access on a (sporadically
working) computer inside. The
menu features burgers, pizza,
lasagne and some West Indian
dishes, but the location on Anse
de Sables is the main draw.

Bars and clubs

Vieux Fort Swoiree

Downtown Vieux Fort. Saturday night
from around 9pm. Every Saturday
night, the town of Vieux Fort
hosts a Swoiree – a street party
similar to the longer-standing
events in Gros Islet and Anse La
Raye, with food stalls, libations,
music and conversation.

Pointe Sable Beach Resort

Anse de Sables, near Vieux Fort ☎454-
6002. Locals turn out in force
for the *Pointe Sable Beach Resort*'s
Tuesday Karaoke night. The
rest of the week this is a local
favourite for a drink and maybe
some dancing.

The east coast

Churned up by the Caribbean trade winds, the pounding waters of the Atlantic Ocean have carved out a rough and jagged east coast for St Lucia, characterized by cliff-lined shores, a crashing surf and a verdant blanket of banana plants. Several long stretches of the area have been designated as protected conservation zones, including the Man Kòtè Mangrove just north of Vieux Fort, and the Savannes Bay Nature Reserve and the Fregate Islands, which are further north near the quiet fishing community of Micoud. Additionally, scenic walking paths through the Mamiku Gardens at Mon Repos offer a peaceful and shady refuge on a hot day.

Just past the busy fishing village of Dennery, the east coast's main highway swings inland towards Castries. The rolling shoreline north of Dennery, however, is almost wild, crisscrossed by a tangle of rough tracks that lead to the sea and to inland villages in the northern part of St Lucia.

Man Kòtè Mangrove

Man Kòtè's red, white and black mangrove trees serve as a protected feeding ground for bird and marine life (such as egrets, herons, conch and juvenile fish), as well as a buffer between the land and sea swells. The swamps here are dense, and a thin beach hugged by palms and sea grape trees is the only bit of the site you can visit.

Though it's littered with beer cans, picnic remains and ashes from cooking fires (and not a very pleasant spot to swim), the beach is nicely secluded. The traditional practice of charcoal making is still practised here, in smouldering pits in the mangrove.

Savannes Bay Nature Reserve

The Savannes Bay Nature Reserve is basically a large mangrove swamp surrounding a pretty bay enclosed by

▲ MAN KÒTÈ MANGROVE

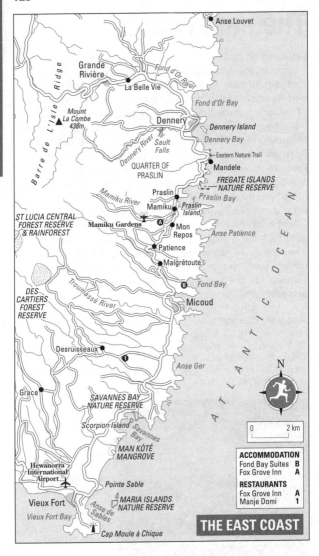

THE EAST COAST

ACCOMMODATION
Fond Bay Suites **B**
Fox Grove Inn **A**

RESTAURANTS
Fox Grove Inn **A**
Manje Domi **1**

Saltibus Point to the north and Burgot Point to the south; small Scorpion Island sits at the north end of the cove. Sheltered by an outlying reef, Savannes Bay forms a protected breeding area for spiny lobsters, conch and numerous species of fish, and it's a prime fishing spot as well. Though there are no walking trails or organized activities in the area, fishermen selling their catch at the small market on the highway might be persuaded

▲ SAVANNES BAY NATURE RESERVE

to take you around the bay to see the swamp from a different perspective.

Honeymoon Beach

If you take the dirt road on the right (ocean side) just past the local winemaker's stand, you'll come to a secluded, little-used beach that's a good spot for a picnic or a snooze, though not for swimming, as the surf is very rough.

Micoud

Spreading back from the pretty, sheltered bay of Port Micoud, the relatively sizeable town

▼ CHARLES LOUIS'S WINE STAND

of Micoud is dotted with fishing boats. The village is best known as the birthplace of the island's first prime minister, John Compton (though there's nothing to commemorate the connection), and as a particularly enthusiastic focal point for two island-wide religious festivals: La Rose in August and La Marguerite in October (see p.158).

Mamiku Gardens

A few minutes' drive north of Micoud ☎455-3729, ⊛www.mamiku.com. Daily 9am–5pm. EC$15, EC$20 with tour. Fifteen-acre Mamiku Gardens is resplendent with brightly coloured exotic blooms, such as hibiscus, ginger and heliconia; tree species include the carambola and gommier (the area's distinctive dugout fishing boats are fashioned from the latter). You can explore the gardens via a simple network of short walking trails, each with resting spots

Locally made wine

At a roadside stand on the righthand-side of the road before you reach Micoud (if you are heading north), you can sample local vintner Charles Louis's **home-made wines**. Louis uses St Lucian tropical fruits like mango and pineapple to create his unusual libations, which are worth tasting at least for their novelty.

Early settlers

The suitability of Micoud's harbour to fishing, and the ready availability of fresh water from the Troumassé River, which borders the town to the south, are the principal factors cited by archeologists as evidence of intense **Amerindian** presence in the area. Some nine settlements are believed to have existed in the Micoud Quarter, and to have been rapidly abandoned after the arrival of the Europeans.

at suitably beautiful points. One five-minute trail leads to the top of a hill that holds the foundations of the former estate's plantation house and provides extraordinary views of nearby Praslin Bay. If you don't stop to admire the scenery, the longest trail will take about twenty minutes to walk. Pick up a free brochure and map at the entrance, or ask someone to guide you through the trails (EC$5 extra). Though the paths themselves are short, there's a lot to see, and you'll probably spend a couple of hours exploring.

Praslin Bay

Sheltered Praslin Bay, a lovely 2km-wide cove split in two by a rocky outcrop, offers a pleasing vista and one of the southeast's few opportunities for a safe ocean swim. Blessed with a gentle surf and plenty of shade, the beach, protected by the narrow bay entrance and enclosed by high hills, is popular with young locals and is especially busy on holidays and weekends. If you're driving, you'll have to find a space at the side of the highway before following one of several paths leading down a precipitous embankment to the beach.

The settlements around Praslin Bay are noted for their distinctive fishing boats, carved out from whole gommier tree trunks and distinguished by their upturned, pointed bows; there are usually a few moored at the small pier in the centre of the bay. Towards the middle of the bay, tiny, unoccupied Praslin Island can normally be visited with an authorized guide from the St Lucia National Trust. However, thanks to the recent construction that's begun on a luxury resort, a vacation condominium community and an eighteen-hole golf course on the bay, tours to Praslin Island, the Fregate Islands Nature Reserve and access to

From battleground to botanical garden

French Governor de Micoud came to own an estate on what is now **Mamiku Gardens** in 1766 ("Mamiku" is probably a Creolized contraction of his wife's name, Madame de Micoud). By 1796, however, the property had fallen into the hands of the British, who used it as a military post and command centre for engaging the Brigands, fugitive slaves who roamed the countryside fighting for freedom. In one of the larger skirmishes, the British fought the Brigands on the estate grounds; as recounted in the diary of Captain de Marchay, fifteen British soldiers died and twenty were wounded, and the estate home was burned to the ground. Shamed by the decisive defeat and loss of British lives, de Marchay later committed suicide. The property was eventually abandoned, and its buildings were left in ruins until the start of the twentieth century, when it became a commercial banana and tropical flower plantation. The botanical gardens are a relatively new addition.

▲ FREGATE ISLANDS NATURE RESERVE

the Eastern Nature Trail (see below) have been temporarily (and possibly permanently) suspended.

Fregate Islands Nature Reserve

The northern section of Praslin Bay. St Lucia National Trust ☎452-5005, ⊛www.slunatrust.org/. Daily Aug–April 9am–5pm; tours only. EC$55. Sunlink Tours ☎1-800-SUNLINK or ☎456-9100, ⊛www.sunlinktours.com. Temporarily closed; call for update.
The Fregate Islands Nature Reserve encompasses a slice of the coastline and two tiny cays just metres offshore, which are named for the seagoing frigate bird that nests here between May and July. The reserve is home to several other bird species, including herons; yellow-eyed, brown-feathered tremblers; and St Lucia orioles – black with orange patches on the belly and underside of the wings. One of St Lucia's larger snakes, a dark tan boa constrictor known locally as *tête chien*, and which often attains a length of four metres, is also occasionally seen in the reserve. Tan with orange, diamond-shaped markings, the poisonous fer de lance snake is found in isolated sections of the east coast (like the reserve) as well, but you're extremely unlikely to ever see these shy creatures. St Lucia's indigenous lizard, the *zandoli tè*, can also be found here.

You're not allowed onto the islands themselves, but the mainland section of the reserve can be explored via an easy 1.5km walking trail (guided walks only). The trail loops through a changing landscape of thick vegetation to dry spots of low-lying bushes and cacti, passing a waterfall that flows in the rainy season, a mangrove swamp and an observation point overlooking the islands before returning to the starting point.

Eastern Nature Trail

Signposted start of the trail lies a few minutes north of the Fregate Islands' interpretative centre. Heritage Tours ☎458-1726 or 451-6058 or 458-1587 or 452-5067, ⊛www

The frigate bird

Also known as the "magnificent frigate" or the "man-o'-war bird", the frigate's two-metre wingspan allows it to soar and swoop for great lengths of time, and it's even believed that it sleeps while floating on air currents. Glossy jet-black birds with forked tail feathers, male frigates have distinctive red or bright orange throat pouches, which expand during mating time to attract females.

The frigate lacks the oily plumage film that allows other seabirds to shed water and resurface after diving, so, rather than risk drowning after a plunge into the ocean, it feeds by skimming the water's surface for fish, or simply by stealing from other birds.

.heritagetoursstlucia.com. EC$10, plus EC$60 guide fee (for up to 15 people). Sunlink Tours ☎ 1-800-SUNLINK or ☎ 456-9100, ⊛ www.sunlinktours.com. Temporarily closed; call for update. Stretching north from Praslin Bay, the 5.5km guided hike along the Eastern Nature Trail runs towards Dennery through some stunning wilderness coastline, and often affords sightings of as many as 38 species of bird, including the magnificent frigate.

Dennery

The village of Dennery extends back from the deep and protected Dennery Bay, with uninhabited Dennery Island at its northern tip. A major export centre for agricultural produce throughout the nineteenth century, Dennery remains a farming community, and is also one of St Lucia's busiest fishing centres.

The town itself is a jumble of compact streets with a few bars, and nothing much in the way of tourist attractions; on Saturday nights, however, the place comes alive with a fish fry on the waterfront – a pleasant, low-key event.

Sault Falls

The Sault Falls (also known as the Errard Falls and the Dennery Falls) are among the tallest and prettiest on the island; a large swimming pool is below and a pleasant picnic area is nearby. You need a 4WD to reach the falls, or, alternatively, you can take an organized tour (see p.148) that includes a visit

▲ DENNERY

▲ FOX GROVE INN

to the farm and plantation house on the sprawling Errand Estate, which is otherwise closed to the public.

Accommodation

Fond Bay Suites

Fond Bay ☎714-1177, ⊛www .fondbaysuites.com. These suites and villas on a secluded property overlook the sweeping beach at Fond Bay and feature all the modern conveniences; some villas have a private pool. A seven-night mimum stay is required Dec 15–Jan 15; a three-night minimum stay is required otherwise. Suites $105, one-bedroom villas $275.

Fox Grove Inn

Mon Repos ☎455-3800, ⊛www .foxgroveinn.com. Set high in the hills several kilometres south of Dennery and about a ten-minute drive north of Vieux Fort, this charming country inn within walking distance of Mamiku Gardens features spectacular views of Praslin Bay and the Fregate Islands. There's a swimming pool, a pool table and lots of walking paths, plus the restaurant is renowned for its excellent local and international cuisine. Rates include breakfast. Double $55, one-bedroom villa $595 per week.

Restaurants

Fox Grove Inn

Mon Repose ☎455-3271. Daily 8–10am, 12.30–2.30pm & 7–10pm. With great views of the banana-and-cocoa clad hills, the Atlantic coastline and the protected Fregate Islands, this is a relaxing spot for moderately priced alfresco lunches or special dinners. The expertly prepared meals include creative salads, delicious pastas and guaranteed-fresh fish from nearby Praslin Bay.

Manje Domi

Desruisseaux ☎455-0729. Daily 8am–11pm. This unexpected find serves tasty and filling Creole food, focusing on very fresh Atlantic fish and hearty local breakfasts. Unfortunately, *Manje Domi* is located on a horrifically potholed sideroad, about 3km off the main highway; neverthe-less, both the restaurant and the cosy bar are popular with locals. Reservations are essential for dinner.

The central interior

St Lucia's vast, mountainous interior is uninhabited, save for a few small forest hamlets on its outer fringes. Arrestingly beautiful and eerily serene – laced with streams and waterfalls, full of exotic flora and fauna and largely untouched by human hand – the forests here offer an absorbing alternative to the sun-and-beach culture of the island's coastal resorts.

Large tracts of the interior have been designated as forest reserves, established to protect the island's last remaining acres of virgin wood and the animals and birds that inhabit them. There are no roads through the interior, but its mountains and forests are criss-crossed by hiking trails, most of which follow old trading routes from St Lucia's colonial days. Of these, the easiest, both in terms of access and level of difficulty, are probably the Union Nature Trail and the Barre de L'Isle Trail, which meanders for almost 2km along the north–south ridge that bisects the island. More strenuous outings take you through St Lucia's tropical rainforests; near Morne Gimie (the island's highest peak); and to the summit of Piton Flore, rewarding climbers with stunning views into the hidden valleys of the interior.

Union Agricultural Station

⊕450-2231/2375. Daily 8am–4.30pm. EC$25. The forestry department's field headquarters – about half an hour's drive north of Castries – is the starting point for the short, easy Union Nature Trail; the complex also contains a herb garden, a small zoo and an interpretive centre with information on endangered indigenous species, vegetation zones and the like. Inside the main office building, rangers are usually on-site every day between 11.30am and 3pm to give tours of the centre and the walking trails, but you're free to amble about by yourself as well.

The station's tiny and tidy zoo houses some fifty animals common to St Lucia and the Caribbean, but it's a sad affair, with animals pacing, jabbering and generally looking distressed. Inmates include vervet monkeys, light grey in colour with a dark facial "mask", several boa constrictors, a couple of agoutis and birds such as macaws, orange-winged parrots and the St Lucia Parrot (or *jacquot*; see box, p.137); as the island's national bird is rarely seen in the wild, this might be your best opportunity to view one – albeit a rather confused and dishevelled one – up close.

To get to the station from Rodney Bay, head south on the Castries–Gros Islet Highway for about ten minutes, turning inland toward Babonneau along the signposted Allan Bousquet Highway. There are no signs to signify that you've reached

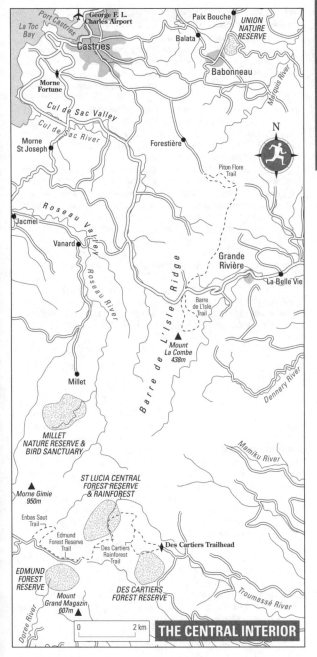

THE CENTRAL INTERIOR

0   2 km

Hiking practicalities

The **Forestry and Lands Department** (Head office at Union Nature Reserve, ☎468-5645 or 450-2231, ✉www.slumaffe.org) maintains St Lucia's protected forest reserves and all of the hiking trails within them. It also determines public access (some parts of the interior are restricted) and provides trained **hiking guides**. Most of the trails require accompaniment by a forest ranger, and advanced booking is essential (see p.155). Additionally, it's unwise to hike the trails alone due to the rise of crime on the island, so be sure to always let someone know where you are going and perhaps carry a cell phone. A flat fee of EC$25 covers admission to a single trail as well as the services of a guide. Accompanied hikes on the longer cross-island tracks (Jungle Hiking Trail, Central Rainforest Trail, and Piton Flore Trail) cost EC$62.50/US$30 per person.

All of the trails described in this chapter can be reached by ordinary rental car or taxi; some can also be accessed by public transport, though bus service is sporadic to small inland villages. If you are travelling by bus or taxi, getting a lift back to town will be difficult unless you arrange a pick-up in advance. Opting for a commercial tour instead (see p.148) simplifies travel to the trailhead, but you may have to share the experience with up to twenty other people (you can confirm the group size before booking). Because the forestry department is understaffed (ranger stations at the start of the trails are sometimes unmanned) and, at times, poorly organized, you should always call a few days in advance to make arrangements.

It's important to remember that although you're in the mountains, it will be hot while you're hiking, so be sure to bring sunscreen and a hat as well as plenty of drinking water and some snacks. Light clothing is best and sturdy footwear is a must for all hikes. During the rainy season (June–Oct), wet-weather gear is a good idea.

the site, but after a winding 2.5km you'll see a large fence to the right, which protects the station's agricultural propagation field; turn right at its end to reach the centre.

Union Nature Trail

The Union Nature Trail begins just to the left of the agricultural station and loops through dry forest, taking about an hour if you don't make too many stops. At only 1.6km, it's an undemanding stroll, with gentle slopes rising to 100m and occasional hillocks to scramble. It's simple to follow and you don't need a guide; free pamphlets that explain some of the flora along the trail are available from the rangers, and common trees such as almond, glory cedar, gommier

and calabash are labelled with plaques.

You might, however, want some expert ranger input when walking the shorter path just behind the station, which winds through a small medicinal garden where rangers grow herbs used in traditional cures. The *wallwort* leaf, for example, is boiled with milk and imbibed for colds and fever, and the *kasialata* leaf can be rubbed on the skin to stop itching.

Barre de L'Isle Trail

Ranger Station ☎453-3242 or Forestry Department ☎468-5645 or 450-2231. Mon–Fri 8.30am–4.30pm. EC$25. The Barre de L'Isle Trail wends its way along the north–south ridge that bisects the island. Walking the trail is a worthwhile morning or afternoon adventure and provides a good taste of St Lucia's diverse topography, flora and fauna, and also affords some expansive views.

Extending about 2km into the forest (you retrace your steps on the way back), the trail is a steep but relatively undemanding

▲ BOA CONSTRICTOR

two-hour hike that alternates between cool, thick forests – where the canopies of towering trees block out most of the sunlight – and wide-open hilltops that provide remarkable views of the coast and of the densely forested interior mountain ranges, including Morne Gimie to the south. The 438-metre Mount La Combe lies near the start of the trail, and you can extend your hike another couple of hours by

Forest flora and fauna

The **topography** of St Lucia's forest reserves is immensely varied, ranging from relatively flat plateaus to steep summits. The peaks and valleys of the central mountains are covered by rich, green woodlands, and the high mountain altitudes create nourishing rain and mist, generating prolific semi-rainforest woodlands and primordial "montane" **rainforests**. These nearly 20,000 acres of rainforest, which comprise about thirteen percent of St Lucia's total landmass, host mammoth trees whose mossy branches groan with epiphytic bromeliads, orchids and even mushrooms; they also feature giant ferns, twisting lianas and numerous other tree and plant species, like the beautiful tropical ginger lily.

Making their homes among the area's trees – which include the indigenous and ubiquitous **gommier** and **chatagnier** varieties – are numerous species of **birds**, of which the most famous is the **St Lucia parrot**, or *jacquot* (*Amazona versicolor*), recognizable by the brilliant blue feathers on its head, the red spot at its breast and its green wings and yellow tail. In the past, the *jacquot* was often hunted for its feathers, and its population reached a low of 150 by the late 1970s. Conservation programmes were initiated in 1978, and today there are thought to be more than 350 *jacquot* living here. Some of the other birds found in the reserves are the **white-breasted thrasher**, the **St Lucia Oriole** and the **St Lucia Peewee**.

Though their numbers have been reduced by hunting, the most common **mammals** in the forests are the shy **agouti**, a rabbit-sized rodent with muscular hind legs, and the cat-sized **manicou**, an opossum with a long snout and a rat-like tail. Other creatures include rats, mice, snakes like boa constrictors and the **mongoose**, a ferret-like animal that feeds on smaller rodents, snakes and domestic fowl, originally introduced to St Lucia to deal with the **fer de lance**, the island's only poisonous snake (rarely seen). There are also reptiles like the endemic St Lucia **tree lizard** and the **pygmy gecko**, tiny and light green; dark brown and black with a row of spiny protrusions along the neck, the prehistoric-looking **iguana** grows to as long as 2m and is found in trees, where it feeds on leaves and fruits.

electing to climb it. As you'd expect, the mountain trail is steep in places, but the reward for your effort is panoramic views that stretch south, east and west.

The signposted start of the Barre de L'Isle strikes into the forest directly from the central Castries–Dennery Highway. Opposite the sign, a gravel road leads up a hillock to the rangers' hut, where you pay your entrance fee and hire a guide. The hut is usually staffed, but an escort isn't strictly necessary for this easy-to-follow walk (though it's recommended for safety reasons). A guide will also be able to identify bird species as well as trees and plants along the trail.

The Edmund Forest Reserve Trail

Forestry Department ☎ 468-5645 or 450-2231 to arrange a hike. Daily 8am–4pm. Guide required. EC$25 per trail. The only way to explore the Edmund Forest Reserve, which spreads over the south-western interior, is on a somewhat strenuous ten-kilometre, three-and-a-half-hour guided hike. Traversing the heart of the island to the open western plains, the trail affords wonderful views along the way, including a spectacular vista of Morne Gimie. Starting early is advisable: you'll benefit from the cool of the morning, and it's a good idea to allow plenty of time for stops.

The trail, which is mostly over flat terrain, with some small streams and crevices spanned by footbridges, provides lots of birdwatching opportunities – keep your eyes open for the rare *jacquot*, as well as orioles, white-breasted thrashers and various hummingbirds. For much of the time, you're in the shadow of Morne Gimie, while in some spots the panoramas of the mountains are vast. Several alternative routes branch off from the main Edmund Trail, with some leading towards the south and others to Morne Gimie. If you want to tackle the latter, you'll need a specialist guide, which can be arranged at

▼ NEAR THE BARRE DE L'ISLE TRAIL

▲ DES CARTIERS RAINFOREST TRAIL

the ranger station – however, it's an arduous and time-consuming hike that isn't often attempted.

The drive to the Edmund Forest Reserve will take about an hour from Soufrière, and if it hasn't rained recently you should be able to make it in a regular rental car. From Soufrière, take the inland road to Fond St Jacques, a tiny rural community (don't expect to be able to stock up on food and drink here) and the last village before the road becomes little more than a track leading only to the rainforest. Buses from Soufrière go only as far as here, so you'll have to walk the remaining 5km to the start of the trail.

After a twenty- to thirty-minute drive, depending on the condition of the road, a wooden ranger station is the first indication that you're in the reserve itself and at the start of the trail; it's usually staffed by forestry guides and officers who will collect your entrance fee. A guide is required by the Forestry Department for all hikes; side trails branch off the main route and it is easy to get lost. Though you may be able to hire a guide at the ranger station, it's best to make arrangements through the Forestry Department at Union

Agricultural Station a few days in advance (☎450-2231/2375). If you elect to walk the whole trail across the island to the east coast, you'll need to plan for someone to drop you at the start and collect you at the end, at Mahaut. Alternatively, if you've got your own transport, you can simply park at the trailhead and turn back when you're ready.

Enbas Saut Falls Trail

To the immediate left of the ranger station at the Edmund Forest Reserve, a sign marks the start of the Enbas Saut Falls Trail, a moderate-to-strenuous 4km loop trail cut that passes through rainforest, cloud forest and elfin woodland vegetation and leads to a couple of spectacular falls, with clean, deep pools for swimming. You can walk the trail alone or with a guide; ask at the ranger station for further information.

Des Cartiers Rainforest Trail

Ranger Station ☎454-5589 or Forestry Department ☎468-5645 or 450-2231. Daily 8.30am–3pm. EC\$25. Found within the Des Cartiers Forest Reserve, the easy, 4km Des Cartiers Rainorest Trail provides a good introduction to St Lucia's interior riches. The well-marked hike follows old military roads laid by the French during World War II, and a guide isn't necessary.

More than 300m above sea level throughout, the trail is a mostly flat, looping hike that skirts the Canelles River and brings you back to the ranger station in about two hours. There are several marked lookout spots, said to be haunts of the *jacquot*, and sweeping views can be had of the south and east coasts from a couple of higher elevation points. At the northern stage of the loop, you'll find the marked turnoff for the Edmund Forest Reserve Trail, which is reached via the Central Rainforest Trail (see next).

The Des Cartiers Forest Reserve lies some ten kilometres into the mountains from the east coast highway, and the trail begins at a small, sporadically staffed Forestry Department interpretive centre where you pay your entrance fee and can peruse the displays on rainforest plant species; toilets and a roofed picnic hut are adjacent. The primary route into the rainforest is a well-signposted turnoff a minute or so north of the east coast village of Micoud (see p.129). The road is in good condition, passing through the tiny hamlet of Anbre and running parallel to a small branch of the Canelles River. (Locals swim in the water, but as it's polluted, taking a dip is not really advisable.) From the main road at Micoud, it's a 10km, thirty-minute drive to the boundary of the reserve.

Buses into the interior from the eastern side are extremely infrequent, and if you don't have a rental car, you're best off hiring a taxi if you want to walk the Des Cartiers Trail. You'll pay about EC$70 one-way from Vieux Fort, for example, where you'll find accommodation and other services, and you should arrange for the driver to wait or come back and collect you.

The Central Rainforest Trail

Union Agricultural Station ☎ 468-5645 or 450-2231. EC$62.50/US$30 per person). The 8km Central Rainforest Trail, which takes about four hours to hike, starts at the Des Cartiers trailhead and

▼ CENTRAL RAINFOREST TRAIL

crosses the island east to west to connect with the Edmund Forest Reserve Trail. There is little traffic on the inland road, and you will need to arrange transportation to the Des Cartiers trailhead and to be collected at the end of the trail.

Piton Flore Trail

Forestiere Ranger station ☎ 451-6168; or Forestry Department ☎ 468-5645 or 450-2231. EC$62.50/US30 per person The strenuous 10km Piton Flore Trail runs north to south, from Forestiere up and over the summit of Piton Flore, and passes through unspoiled rainforest, filled with ferns, fig trees and more. It comes out on the main highway at the Barre de L'Isle trailhead from where it's easy to catch a bus back to Castries or Rodney Bay (except perhaps on Sunday, when service is less frequent). Alternatively, you can go up Piton Flore and then retrace your steps back to Forestiere (8km/5m).

The Jungle Hiking Trail

Forestry Department ☎ 468-5645 or 450-2231. EC$62.50/US$30 per person. The Jungle Hiking Trail

(16km/10m) is a long (at least six hours), demanding hike starting at the Barre de L'Isle trailhead and running south, down the mountainous spine of the island through the blank spot on the map to join up with the the Edmund Forest Reserve Trail near Soufrière. While it is easy to get a public bus to the Barre de L'Isle trailhead, you will need to arrange to be picked up at the Edmund Forest Reserve Ranger Station at the end.

▲ PITON FLORE TRAIL

PLACES The central interior

Essentials

Arrival

Except for those coming from elsewhere in the Caribbean, all international flights arrive at **Hewanorra International Airport** near Vieux Fort at the southern tip of the island. Intra-Caribbean flights mainly land at the **George F.L. Charles Airport** in Castries. Rental cars, taxis and buses are available at both airports (though bus service to Soufrière from Hewanorra and Vieux Fort is irregular). Some hotels offer free airport shuttles; ask when you book.

From October to May, major **cruise lines** dock almost daily at Port Castries,

within walking distance of Downtown, and smaller lines also dock at Soufrière. Taxis meet ships arriving in both spots, and ferries and buses heading north to Rodney Bay or south to Vieux Fort are only a short walk away.

You can also reach St Lucia by high-speed passenger **ferry** from Martinique, Guadeloupe or Dominica via Cox and Co. Ltd (Corner of Jeremie and Cadet sts, Castries, ☎ 456-5000/5022, ☜ www .express-des-iles.com).

Information and maps

The **St Lucia Tourist Board** maintains several offices abroad, and it's worth contacting them before your trip for free maps and general information. The Board's main office on the island is inconveniently located about a mile north of Downtown Castries at the Sureline Building, just after the roundabout on the road to Gros Islet (PO Box 221, Castries, St Lucia, WI ☎ 452-4094 or 452-5968, ☜ www.stlucia.org). There are also tourist information kiosks at both airports, the Pointe Seraphine and La Place Carenage shopping complexes in Castries and on the waterfront in Soufrière (see p.103).

Other useful sources for up-to-date local information are the free, visitor-oriented publications available from the tourist board and various hotels across the island. *Tropical Traveller* (☜ www .tropicaltraveller.com) is a monthly magazine with maps, restaurant and nightlife listings and lots of suggestions for things to see and do. The annual glossy magazine *Visions* (☜ www.slucia.com/visions) and the pocketsize *Paradise* (☜ www .paradisestlucia.com), published twice a year, offer more of the same with the addition of hotel listings.

Maps

You can pick up free St Lucia **maps** at tourist offices, hotels and car rental offices or you can download them at ☜ www.skyviews.com or ☜ www .caribbean-on-line.com; if you plan to do some exploring on secondary roads or hiking in the interior, you'll need more detailed maps. The best available is the 1:50,000 Ordnance Survey tourist map, available from bookshops or map specialists. In the UK try Stanfords, 12–14 Long Acre, London WC2E 9LP (for mail order call ☎ 020/7836 1321 or see ☜ www.stanfords.co.uk) and in the US try Rand McNally (for mail order or your nearest outlet call ☎ 1-800/275-7263 or log on to ☜ www .randmcnally.com). The Survey and Mapping Section of the St Lucia Ministry of Planning, Development, Environment and Housing (1st floor, Greaham Louisy Administration Building, John Compton Hwy, Castries ☎ 468-5030/5020) will sell you a black-and-white photocopy of a 1:50,000 map – if they have the large paper to print it on.

Getting around

While the more populated parts of St Lucia – like the Castries to Gros Islet corridor on the northwest coast and the Castries to Vieux Fort road across the island – are well connected by buses, more remote areas are accessible only to those with their own transport.

Buses

If you're relaxed enough to cope with long waiting times and frequent stops along routes, travelling by **bus** is probably the most convenient and economical way to get around, with fares to anywhere on the island costing EC$10 or less. St Lucia's buses, which are actually minivans, are identifiable by an "H" on the licence plate. Schedules are not set, and most drivers wait until the bus is full before setting off. As a general rule, services between major towns run every thirty to sixty minutes from about 6am until 10pm on weekdays, with an extended timetable on Fridays to and from the Gros Islet Jump Up and to the Fish Fry in Anse La Raye. There is a reduced timetable on Saturdays and practically no buses run on Sundays. Small cement pavilions serve as **bus stops**, but if you flag a bus down anywhere along a route it will probably stop if it isn't jammed full.

Taxis

Taxis – identifiable by their red licence plates with the letters "TX" – are in plentiful supply. You'll see them cruising for fares on the streets of the main towns, and at obvious locations such as airports and tourist spots like Pigeon Island and Reduit Beach. Though all taxis are unmetered, **fares** are set by the government and drivers are required to carry a rate sheet in their car. It's always best to confirm the fare before getting in. Typical rates from Hewanorra Airport are: EC$150 to Castries, EC$180 to Rodney Bay and EC$160 to Soufrière. Castries to Rodney Bay is EC$50, Castries to Soufrière is EC$160, and Rodney Bay to Gros Islet is EC$20. Taxis also offer **guided tours** for around US$20 per hour (for as many as four people), or US$140 for a full day, but, unlike standard fares, this rate is often negotiable.

Cars

The ideal way to traverse the island is to rent a **car**. As well as giving you complete independence, it's ultimately less expensive than taxi travel if you intend to do much exploring.

Car rental **rates** start at US$45 per day for a compact, manual-shift vehicle without air conditioning and go as high as US$90 for a luxury model. Jeeps and other 4WD vehicles range from US$65 to US$100. Although the main round-the-island highway has been resurfaced over the past couple of years and is for the most part in good repair, some stretches are still peppered with king-size potholes; renting a **4WD** is highly recommended. Off the main highway, some destinations are reachable *only* by 4WD, and secondary roads are, in general, appallingly bad.

While mileage is unlimited, rates don't include **petrol**, which at time of writing costs around EC$8.50 per imperial gallon. (Note that most gas stations are cash-only.) You need to be **aged 21** or over to rent a car, and some companies require a minimum age of 25. You'll also need to have a **temporary St Lucia driver's licence** (EC$30 for one day or EC$54 for a three-month permit), which you can get at the Immigration office at the airport before you line up to clear customs, at a police station, or at some of the rental agencies when you pick up your car (ask when you book).

Car rental agencies

Alto Gros Islet ☎452-0233, Hewanorra Airport ☎454-5311, ⊛www.altorentacar.com.

Avis Castries ☎452-2202, Hewanorra Airport ☎454-6325, George F.L. Charles Airport ☎452-2046, ⊛www.avis.com.

Ben's Westcoast Jeep and Taxi Services Bridge St, Soufrière ☎459-5457/7160, ⊛www.westcoastjeeps.com, VHF Radio Ch 16.

Budget Castries ☎452-9887; Hewanorra Airport ☎454-7470; ⊛www.budget stlucia.net.

Cool Breeze Soufrière, Rodney Bay, and both airports ☎459-7729, ⊛www .coolbreezecarrental.com.

Courtesy Rodney Bay ☎452-8140, ⊛www.courtesycarrentals.com.

Guy's George F.L. Charles Airport ☎451-7885.

Hertz Hewanorra Airport ☎454-9636, George F.L. Charles Airport ☎451-7351, ⊛hertz@candw.lc, ⊛www.hertz.com.

Holiday and Business Car Rental Rodney Bay ☎452-0872, ⊛www .hbcarrentals.com.

Rent-A-Ride Rodney Bay ☎452-9404/0732, ⊛www.vcrentals.com.

St Lucia National Car Rental Hewanorra Airport, G.F.L. Charles Airport, Pointe Seraphine, and Le Sport Hotel ☎450-8721, ⊛skyviews.com/stlucia/slncr

Motorcycles

It is possible to rent a **motorcycle**, but due to hazards such as large potholes, torrential tropical downpours, occasional mudslides, kamikaze bus drivers, roads comprised mainly of hairpin turns (on the west coast) and lazy animals sunbathing in the middle of the road, it is not recommended.

Bicycles

Biking along the main highway around St Lucia is emphatically not recommended. There are no shoulders, visibility is limited around the frequent sharp turns and more than a few people drive too fast and carelessly. In addition, the steep, hilly terrain would wear out even the best riders in short order. There are, however, some mountain biking trails at Anse Mamin in the south as well as guided tours on secondary roads in the northeast (see p.155 for rental details).

Water taxis

In parts of St Lucia you can take advantage of the convenient and fun **water taxis**, mostly used by tourists and especially handy for getting to nearby beaches.

In the Soufrière area, Moby Dick Water Taxi (☎ 459-5651 or ☎ 484-6224) shuttles passengers from the town's waterfront to and from many of the beaches in the area and up the west coast as far as Castries (see p.101 for details). In Castries harbour, water taxis ferry passengers (mainly from the cruise ships) between the Pointe Seraphine shopping complex and Downtown's docks. In Marigot Bay, a twenty-four hour ferry shuttles back and forth between the

---

Driving in St Lucia

Driving in St Lucia is not for the faint of heart. Less than half of St Lucia's 800km of paved roads are on flat land and there may not be a single 500m of straight road on the entire island, which does not deter some drivers from overtaking laggards on a blind turn. The **west and south coast road** from Cap Estate in the north to Vieux Fort in the south is in excellent shape but full of twists and turns and steep hills; during the rainy season it is vulnerable to mudslides (very quickly and efficiently cleaned up by road crews). Connecting Castries to Vieux Fort via Dennery, the **east coast highway** is a good road (though with a few colossal craters, especially around Dennery) and the quickest way to get from the south to the north of the island. In the **north**, the roads that link the east and west coasts are horrifically potholed, generally unmarked and impassable without a 4WD vehicle. Urban driving is also challenging; all towns and villages have a surfeit of one-lane, one-way roads that are clogged with cars parked on both sides, making traffic jams imminent. Secondary roads heading to inland settlements and the rainforest reserves in the **south** are in variable condition. Some – as noted in the text – are in good shape and passable by car. Others will rattle the bolts out of your rental vehicle. The best defence is to rent a 4WD and go slow.

Caribbean island hopping

It's not difficult to use St Lucia as a launch pad for visits to other Caribbean destinations. The nearby islands of Guadeloupe, Martinique and Dominica can be reached by ferry within a couple of hours, and St Lucia-based Sunlink Tours (see below) offers day-trips to the Grenadines. Several pan-Caribbean airlines, like LIAT, Caribbean Star and BWIA (see Directory, p.159) ply routes among the islands, with daily services to and from St Lucia, and also offer discounted multi-destination air passes for those who wish to do some island-hopping.

north and south sides of the bay (a one-minute crossing for EC$5 round trip). It is also possible to take a water taxi from Rodney Bay to Pigeon Island (EC$26 round trip; ticket booth on Reduit Beach Drive ☎452-0087).

Tours

Sunlink Tours (Reduit Drive, Rodney Bay, ☎1-800-SUNLINK or ☎456-9100, ⓦ www.sunlinktours.com) is the largest tour company on the island, offering a wide range of outings that includes boat excursions, helicopter tours, nature hikes, visits to waterfalls and sugar plantations and day-trips to nearby islands; additionally, Sunlink handles bookings for many of the other tour operators on St Lucia. Their costs range from US$40 for a half-day tour to about $80–90 for a full-day trip (prices include transportation to and from your hotel). Alternatively, you can book directly with one of the outfits listed below.

Land tours

Several local companies offer **guided tours** of St Lucia's east coast and central mountains aboard 4WD trucks. Most are half-day or all-day expeditions averaging US$50 or US$80–90 respectively per person, with stops at waterfalls, scenic viewing areas and beaches; some involve rainforest hikes. Lunch, refreshments and admission to selected sites are part of the deal, and you'll be picked up at your hotel. If the size of your group matters to you, confirm the number when you book, as some companies set out with up to forty people. Contact C and M Touring (Gros Islet ☎ 450-0073 or 450-1875 or ☎ 716-1333, ⓦ www .cmtouring.com) or Jungle Tours (☎450-0434, ⓦ www.jungletoursstlucia.com) for more information.

Boat trips

Skimming along the calm waters on St Lucia's lovely west coast, **sightseeing** and **party boats** (usually customized catamarans) offer a great way to view the island's bays and interior mountain peaks. Most excursions include stops for snorkelling and swimming or a visit to a coastal village (usually Soufrière and/or Marigot Bay) as well as lunch and drinks. Note that as the boats are often crowded with rowdy revellers taking advantage of the free-flowing rum, the trip may not be the quiet cruise you anticipated. Most trips depart from Vigie Marina in Castries or Rodney Bay Marina and head south along the coast for half- or full-day cruises, which start at US$40 and US$75 respectively, per person; check whether transport to and from your hotel is included in the price.

Boat tour operators
Carnival Party Cruises ☎452-5586,

@www.carnivalsailing.com. Departs Rodney Bay daily, calling at Marigot Bay and Soufrière.

Endless Summer Cruises ☎450-8651, @www.stluciaboattours.com. Runs full-day tours (Tues & Fri, US$90) out of Rodney Bay to Soufrière, La Soufrière Sulphur Springs and Touraille Waterfalls, with stops at beaches around Anse Cochon for swimming and snorkelling, sightseeing at Marigot Bay and lunch at the Fond Doux cocoa estate. They also offer half-day swimming jaunts to various spots along the northwest coast.

Mango Tango ☎452-0459. A catamaran operating out of Rodney Bay shuttles snorkellers to various west coast spots. A larger, all-inclusive tour takes in Soufrière's sulphur springs and the Diamond Botanical Gardens and waterfall, with lunch at the Still Plantation near Soufrière.

Mystic Man Tours Soufrière ☎459-7783, @www.mysticmantours.com. One of the few tour companies departing from the south of the island, offering whale- and dolphin-watching tours with small groups; glass-bottom boat tours; half- and full-day sailing trips; sport-fishing expeditions; shopping trips to Castries by boat; and sunset cruises.

Unicorn ☎ 452-6811, @www.brigunicorn.com. Featured in the movies *Roots* and *Pirates of the Caribbean*, the *Unicorn* is a picturesque 140-foot replica of an eighteenth-century tall ship, making enjoyable and popular expeditions from Rodney Bay to Soufrière with sightseeing stops en route.

Wave Riders ☎452-0808 or 485-3527 Offers day-trips to nearby Martinique, which include sightseeing, shopping, snorkelling and an on-board barbecue. Departs daily from Rodney Bay Marina ar 7:30am for the 90min trip to Martinique and returns at 5:30pm. Register by noon the day before.

Heritage Tours

The Heritage Tourism Association of St Lucia (HERITAS) has established more than a dozen **Heritage Tours**, which offer unique cultural experiences and promote community involvement as well as environmental sustainability. You can book through the HERITAS office at La Place Carenage (P.O. Box GM 868, Castries, St Lucia, West Indies ☎458-1726/451-6058/458-1587/452-5067, @www.heritagetoursstlucia.com) or directly with individual tour operators. With the exception of the guided hikes listed, you can also buy tickets on-site, though calling ahead is strongly recommended.

Tour attractions

Balenbouche Estate (see p.118)
Castries Heritage Walk (see p.131)
Eastern Nature Trail (see p.131)
Fond Doux Estate (see p.108)
Fond Latisab Creole Park (see p.87)
Grand Anse Turtle Watch (see p.85)
Gros Piton/Fond Gens Libre Trail (see p.107)
Mamiku Gardens (see p.129)
Piton Flore Rainforest Hike (see p.141)
St Lucia Folk Research Centre (see p.56)
Toraille Waterfall (see p.104)

Aerial tours

Breathtaking aerial tours of the island are offered by St Lucia Helicopters (☎453-6950, @ www.stluciahelicopters.com), with various trips ranging from US$55 per person to US$130 per person.

Media

St Lucia has three national **newspapers**: the *Star* (@www.stluciastar.com) is published on Mon, Wed & Fri; the *Voice* comes out on Tues, Thurs & Sat; and the weekly *St Lucia Mirror* (@www.stluciamirroronline.com) is available on Fridays. The *Voice* was established in 1885, making it one of the oldest newspapers in the region. Its entertainment section is good for local events, while the *Star* tends to be the more complete all-around hard news source. A regional weekend newspaper, *One Caribbean* (@ www.onecaribbean.com), serves Grenada, Dominica, St Lucia and St Vincent, while the *Crusader* is a free paper with some news and local events.

The public **radio** station here is Radio St Lucia (97.7 FM, 660 AM), while the station of choice among local bus drivers appears to be Rhythm FM (94.5), which plays Caribbean and international soul music interspersed with local chat.

Mid-range and upscale hotels generally have access to satellite-fed international cable **television** stations, including HBO and some British, French and Spanish channels. On cable channels 2, 34 and 35, respectively, the local stations NTV (National Television Network), HTS (Helen Television System, ⊛ www.htsstlucia.com) and DBS (Daher Broadcasting Service) offer news and sports broadcasts, local talk shows, political speeches, riveting televised conferences, fire-and-brimstone religious sermons and some original programmes.

Telephones

St Lucia has a reliable phone system. Public phone booths are located all around the island and take either coins (EC$1 or EC$0.25) or the phone cards available from Cable & Wireless offices, post offices, pharmacies, souvenir stores and convenience shops. Local calls cost EC$0.25 for two minutes and double that for long-distance; phone cards come in denominations of EC$40, EC$20 and EC$10. Some public phones allow you to make long-distance calls using a credit card, but this can be a very expensive method of calling home. Note also that the charges for making direct long-distance calls from your hotel room are exorbitant. To call St Lucia from overseas, use your country's international access code (001 in UK, Ireland and NZ, 1 in the US and Canada, 0011 from Australia), followed by area code 758 and the seven-digit number.

Depending on its make, you may be able to use your cell phone on St Lucia, although it's likely you'll have to take it into a Cable and Wireless, Digicel or Cingular outlet on arrival and have it fitted with a local sim chip to make it functional. (Check with your service provider before you leave home.) Another option is to rent a cell phone for the duration of your trip, which you can do very inexpensively from Cingular (☎ 456-1800) for EC$10 a week, plus an EC$250 security deposit (a credit card imprint will suffice). It is a good idea to reserve a phone in advance of your trip, as they are always in demand. Additionally, you can rent (US$29 a week) or buy (US$300) a phone on St Lucia from USA-based ⊛ www .cellularabroad.com (☎ 1-800-287-3020 in the US). A sim card will be an extra US$79. Cingular has outlets at the JQ Charles Mall in Rodney Bay and on New Dock Road in Vieux Fort. Cable and Wireless (☎ 453-9900) has retail outlets at the Gablewoods Mall in Castries, at the Rodney Bay Marina, and in Vieux Fort.

Costs and money

Though St Lucia is not inexpensive, you can still enjoy yourself even if you're on a budget: decent and even charming accommodation is available at reasonable prices; the bus system is cheap; and farmers markets and cafés around the island offer very affordable and delicious fruit, vegetables, fish and local cuisine.

St Lucia's official currency is the Eastern Caribbean dollar (EC$), which generally trades at a rate of EC$2.68 to US$1; EC$3.27 to €1; and EC$4.72 to £1. In shops, though, the exchange rate will likely be EC$2.50 to US$1, in the vendor's favour. In the case of hotels, car rental, restaurants and practically everything related to tourism, most prices in St Lucia are quoted in both EC and US dollars, as both currencies are accepted virtually island-wide. Most prices in this guide are quoted in EC$, except when noted otherwise (see below).

Major credit cards and US-dollar travellers' cheques are widely accepted in St Lucia, though most small shops, restaurants and simple guesthouses often accept cash only. Cash machines are readily available, especially at the airport and in Downtown Castries, dispensing EC dollars.

Accommodation

Accommodation on the island runs the gamut from a few sprawling all-inclusives to modest bed-and-breakfasts. Most hotels are bunched together around the northern enclave of Rodney Bay; if you crave more charm and seclusion, seek out one of the small hotels and guesthouses tucked discreetly into sandy coves and hillsides along the less trammelled west coast, or even more off the beaten track on the little-visited south and east coasts. The rates quoted in this guide are in US dollars and, unless otherwise indicated, reflect the cheapest double room in high season. Most **hotels** fall into the US$100–150 range. Though it's not illegal, camping on the island is difficult, as it requires obtaining permission from private landowners beforehand.

A fun and cost-effective option for families or other groups is to rent a **villa**. Rates, which run about US$900–4000 per week in high season, sometimes include maid and cooking services. For more information, contact Tropical Villas (PO Box 189, Castries ☎758/450-8240, ⊛www.tropicalvillas.net) or Lucian Leisure (PO Box 1538, Castries ☎ 758/452-8898, ⊛ www.lucian-leisure.com), or check out the extensive listings on the Balenbouche Estate website (⊛ www.balenbouche.com).

Room tax

When booking accommodation, remember that St Lucian hotels generally levy a 10 percent **service charge** and an 8 percent government **accommodation tax** to the bill – a hefty addition for a week's stay even at a medium-priced hotel; the prices quoted in this guide are exclusive of these charges unless otherwise noted.

Food and drink

St Lucia is an island of wonderful food and great cooks. Its rich volcanic soil yields an abundance of luscious tropical fruits and vegetables – including 100 varieties of mangoes – and fresh seafood is plentiful. These flavourful elements are worked into tasty traditional Creole dishes or delightful new creations made with flare by imaginative chefs at island resorts. **Creole cooking** reflects St Lucia's history, mixing the spicy, tomato-based sauces and starchy carbohydrates of African and Indian cooking with inventive garnishes that are a product of the island's French colonial influence. Other cuisines include Asian, French, Mexican, Italian, British and North American, while fast-food fixes are available in the form of burgers, barbecue chicken and pizza.

St Lucia's restaurant scene is dominated by small, reasonably priced eateries with few pretensions, but there are a handful of upmarket establishments offering gourmet fare as well. Most restaurants add a mandatory 10 percent **service charge**, and most accept credit cards; small mom-and-pop operations and roadside food stalls, however, are usually cash only.

For a truly local culinary experience, visit one of the island's weekend **fish fries** – in Anse La Raye and Gros Islet on Friday nights and in Dennery and Vieux Fort on Saturdays. At these street parties you can wander from stall to stall sampling homecooked dishes and local drinks, and then dance it all off.

Some of St Lucia's restaurants are closed on Sundays, except for those affiliated with hotels. Also, during the off-season, **opening hours** might change and some places close for up to a month at a time. While we've given opening hours for most establishments, many spots will stay open as long as they have customers. Others will transport you to and from your hotel at no extra cost. Unless otherwise stated, all restaurant prices are given in EC$.

St Lucia's favourite local libation is the very palatable Piton **beer**, brewed in Vieux Fort (a low-calorie version is also available). A variation called a Piton shandy borrows from the British practice of mixing beer with something sweet – in this case ginger ale. St Lucia also minds a Caribbean tradition by producing fine **rum**. Several brands are available at St Lucia Distillers, but among the best are the Chairman's Reserve, a smooth dark variety, and Denros, a strong white rum. Also on the shelves are Bounty (the island's best seller for its even taste), Five Blondes and Crystal brands. Those with a sweet tooth will appreciate La Belle Creole Black Satin coffee liqueur and Ti Tasse coffee rum liqueur, often mixed in exotic drinks or served after dinner with desserts and coffee. For a more down-to-earth local experience, you could visit a rum shop, which is typically a wooden shack with rustic benches and bar stools. Here you can buy simple groceries, a couple of basic beers, loose cigarettes and a lot of barely drinkable white rum for around EC$1.50. If rum isn't your spirit, you might find whisky, brandy or wine in more upscale establishments.

Distilled **water** is widely available on St Lucia, although the tap water is generally safe to drink. For a cheap and healthy alternative, try **coconut water**: drunk straight from the opened husk of a green nut, the juice is naturally sterilized and rich in potassium and other minerals. You'll find vendors at the markets and roadside stands throughout the island.

St Lucian food glossary

accra deep-fried salted cod fritter
boudin spicy blood sausage
breadfruit starchy, bland fruits (called *bwape* in Creole) that grow on trees and are eaten fried or boiled
brochette skewered and barbecued meats and vegetables
callaloo a leafy green vegetable that looks and tastes like spinach and is often used to make soup
carambola a sweet, star-shaped fruit

chataigne breadfruit-like fruit with large seeds, prepared as a side dish

christophene vegetable with white, watery flesh, eaten boiled or sautéed

colombo meat, usually goat, lamb or chicken, in a spicy curry sauce

dolphin a local, omnipresent and very tasty fish also known as dorado.

dasheen a starchy root vegetable

fig green or ripe bananas

float deep-fried semi-sweet dough, so-named because it floats when fried; eaten as a snack on its own or as a side dish with fish

ground provisions a mixture of boiled starchy vegetables such as plantains, dasheen, christophene, yams and potatoes

jerk method of seasoning meat (usually chicken, pork or fish) with a multi-spice mixture heavy on pepper and pimento

koko coconut in Creole

lambi conch

love apple tropical fruit with pulpy, sweet flesh

mago mango in Creole

mauby a cold sweet drink made with cinnamon bark, believed to be good for detoxifying the body

papaya, pawpaw or papay large orange or yellow fruit high in both vitamins and an enzyme used as a meat tenderizer

pepperpot soup spicy soup of beef and callaloo

plantain a larger, blander member of the banana family that turns from savoury to sweet as it ripens, and is eaten fried or boiled at either stage

roti flat, baked unleavened bread wrapped around a mix of curried vegetables or meat

saltfish salted cod

saltfish and green fig St Lucia's national dish of reconstituted, fried saltfish with cooked green banana

soursop a large, green, rough-skinned fruit that yields white, pulpy and sweet (not sour) flesh

sweetsop a smaller version of a soursop

tamarind a tropical tree that bears the pod from which acidic, sour fruit is eaten; also used to make relish-like syrups, candy and drinks

titiri small fish, deep-fried and eaten whole

ugli a hybrid citrus fruit that's a cross between a grapefruit and a tangerine

Sport and outdoor activities

St Lucia is a great destination for energetic travellers, with a wide variety of outdoor activities both on- and offshore.

Scuba diving

Though not known primarily for its diving opportunities, St Lucia nevertheless has more than enough underwater sights to keep the average diver happy. The best spots for **diving** and **snorkelling** are found on the island's southwestern fringes, where the Soufrière Marine Management Area (T 758/459-5500, W www.smma.org.lc) hugs the shoreline for nearly seven miles from Anse L'Ivrogne to Anse Jambon. The reefs here are pristine by most standards, and the area is protected for fishing and recreational use; the nominal dive fee (US$3 per day or US$10 per year) goes towards the park's upkeep.

If you've never tried scuba diving, it's easy to learn by taking a PADI (Professional Association of Diving Instructors) training course. Known as **resort courses**, these lead you through the basics (usually in a swimming pool) before heading to the ocean for a supervised dive of about 12m. Costs start at US$80. More detailed certification programmes such as open-water, advanced open-water and refresher courses are available through various dive centres for US$200–450.

Beach and ocean safety

St Lucia is near the equator and the sun's rays are very strong even on overcast days – a high SPF sunscreen is therefore essential. St Lucia has some lovely swimming beaches, primarily along the west coast, however the waters around the north and east coasts of the island are wild and full of undertows and currents that will pull you out to sea – making them very dangerous and unsuitable for swimming. Both locals and tourists have died here.

If you're already **certified**, you should of course bring along your card as well as any pieces of equipment you'd rather not rent. Some operators include diving gear in their packages, so it's worth checking beforehand. Prices for certified divers start at about US$50 for a one-tank dive, with night dives costing from US$70. If you're a serious enthusiast, it might be worth looking into packages offered by hotels such as *Anse Chastanet*, *Still Beach Resort* and the *Margot Beach Club*, which bundle flights, accommodation and a specified number of dives at ostensibly discounted rates.

Snorkelling

Reefs around the base of Petit Piton and Anse Chastanet Bay are particularly stunning places to **snorkel**. The **coral varieties** found in St Lucian waters include the sizeable, tan-coloured elkhorn and the soft, purple or green gorgonian, among others. **Fish** are plentiful as well, and some of the most frequent reef visitors are the blue-and-white angelfish (with darkish stripes) and the triggerfish, which is dark green with a yellow belly and an elongated snout.

Many of the island's diving centres rent masks and fins for about US$10 per hour; for about US$20–35 they'll also take you out for an escorted offshore trip, which is a far more rewarding option than striking out alone from the beach.

Watersports operators

Action Adventures Divers *The Still Beach Resort*, Soufrière ☎758/459-5599, ☻www.aadivers.net. Scuba and snorkelling.
Buddies Scuba Rodney Bay Marina ☎758/450-8406, ☻www.buddiesscuba .com. Scuba and snorkelling.

Dive Fair Helen Vigie Marina, Choc Bay, and Margot Bay ☎451-7716, ☻www .divefairhelen.com. Scuba, snorkelling and kayaking.
Frog's Diving at *Harmony Suites*, Rodney Bay, ☎450-8831 or 458-0798, ☻www .frogsdiving.com
Scuba St Lucia *Anse Chastanet Resort* ☎758/459-7755/457-1400, ☻www .scubastlucia.com or ☻www.junglereef adventures.com. Scuba and snorkelling in the Soufrière Marine Management Area and other sites around the island.

Windsurfing

The long stretch of white sand and rolling surf at Anse de Sables near Vieux Fort is popular with **windsurfers**. Tornado Kite and Surf St Lucia on the beach at Anse des Sables (☎758/454-7579, ☻www .tornado-surf.com) offers windsurfing and kitesurfing lessons and rentals. Open Oct–June.

Sailing

Sailing around St Lucia or visiting neighbouring islands aboard a chartered yacht has become increasingly popular in recent years. Costs depend on the size of the group, the length of time you'll be sailing and the size of the yacht, but you can expect to pay about US$6100 per week in high season. If you don't have sailing skills or if you're more interested in relaxing than working, a captain and crew can accompany you for an additional fee: a captain is roughly US$100 per day, and a crew is US$25–30 each per day. You can also hire a cook for about US$60 per day The larger charter companies will arrange holiday packages around yachting, with prices covering charter fees, airfare and accommodation while the boat is being prepared. The most reliable operators include:

Destination St Lucia (Rodney Bay ☎452-8531, ⊛www.dsl-yachting.com), Moorings Yacht Charters (Marigot Bay ☎451-4230; in North America ☎888/922-4811; ⊛www.moorings.com) and Stirrup Yachts (Castries ☎452-8000).

Kayaking

Jungle Reef Adventures (☎457-1400, ⊛www.junglereefadventures.com) offers **kayaking** day-trips in the calm Caribbean Sea along the southwest coast for about US$60. River kayaking as well as coastal day-trips are available for US$60 from Dive Fair Helen (☎451-7716, ⊛www.divefairhelen.com).

Sport fishing

Good game fishing can be found offshore, with main catches including sizeable marlin, kingsfish, wahoo and shark. If you're lucky, you might also hook the rarer tuna, dorado or mackerel. **Deep-sea fishing** excursions run half- or full days, with bait and tackle (and sometimes drinks) included. Full-day trips include lunch; half-days start at about US$300 for as many as six people. To make arrangements, contact Hackshaw's in Castries (☎453-0553, ⊛www.hackshaws.com); Captain Mike's at Vigie Marina (☎452-7044 or 450-1216, ⊛www.captmikes.com); Mako Watersports in Rodney Bay (☎452-0412 or ☎717-9223); or Mystic Man Tours in Soufrière (☎459-7783, ⊛www.mysticmantours.com).

Biking

Mountain biking is available on an old sugarcane estate that fronts Anse Mamin – a small, secluded beach surrounded by forest and accessible only from Anse Chastanet beach (ask at the Scuba St Lucia shop for a free lift) or by hired boat from the Soufrière shore. The forest has twelve miles of custom-built, off-road trails ranging from beginner (suitable for families) to nearly impossible (like Tinker's Trail). The operators, Bike St Lucia (☎459-7755, ⊛www.bikestlucia.com), ensure that you know how to handle their professional equipment before letting you loose for the day to explore the trails and enjoy the eighteenth-century French plantation ruins, fresh-water reservoir and swimming hole. Bike St Lucia offers a full-day taxi/boat package from any hotel in the north of the island for US$75 per person; if you make your own way to the beach at Anse Chastanet, the cost is US$49 per day. Island Bike Hike St Lucia, based in Castries (☎458-0908, ⊛www.cyclestlucia.com), offers a cycling day-trip to the otherwise difficult-to-reach northeast coast through a cocoa estate to Sault Falls, near Dennery, as well as a combined cycling expedition with sightseeing around Soufrière; both tours are US$50 per person.

Hiking

St Lucia's lush, mountainous interior and rugged coastline allow for great **hiking** experiences, and indeed the only way to explore much of the uninhabited central rainforest is on foot. This region – which has an abundance of colourful tropical flora and fauna, winding rivers, spectacular waterfalls and grand vistas from the mountaintops – is crisscrossed with trails maintained by the Forestry Department and local community groups.

You don't necessarily need a guide for many of the hiking trails on the island, although hiring one will help to identify natural attractions, and locals advise that it is unsafe to hike alone due to the threat posed by a small but present criminal element. On some of the longer Forestry trails, guides are mandatory (see p.136 for details), and you'll need advance permission from the Forestry Department's Environmental Education and Ecotourism Unit (office located at Union Forest Reserve ☎450-2231/2331 ext.316/317/318, ⊛www.slumaffe.org.) to enter certain protected areas.

The Forestry Department is based at **Union Agricultural Station**, near Babonneau, and has a short nature trail, an interpretive centre and a zoo on its grounds (see p.134). The Department is responsible for the **Millet Bird Sanctuary**, **Des Cartiers Rainforest Trail**, **EnBas Saut Falls Trail** and **Edmond**

Forest Reserve Trail. The entrance fee for these trails is EC$25, payable at the trailhead. Although the trails are short (2–5km long), well-maintained and easy to follow, a guide is recommended if you are travelling alone. Ranger huts at the trailheads are officially open daily 8.30am–3pm, but some are staffed only sporadically. Longer hikes, like the Central Rainforest Trail and the Jungle Hiking trail (8km and 16km respectively; see p.140 & p.141) require a guide and advance booking and cost EC$60 each.

The St Lucia National Trust (☎ 452-5005, ● www.slunatrust.org) offers guided walks on the **Maria Islands Nature Reserve**, off Anse des Sables, and you can also contact the private tour operator Trim Tours (Sunny Acres, Castries ☎ 452-2502, ● www.trimtours.com) for an excursion to the sanctuary. Additionally, you can hike the northeast coastline either on your own or with a guide, beginning at **Cas-en-Bas** (see p.84 for details). Keith Compton (Marisule, ☎ 452-8134) who has hiked this coastline since childhood – and indeed most forest trails and river valleys on the island in search of undiscovered waterfalls – offers excellent half- and full-day guided hikes (US$120) and tours all over the island.

Community-run Gros Piton Tours (☎ 459-9748 or 489-0136, ● www .grospitontours.com. EC$80) provides very professional guided hikes up **Gros Piton**, a trip that takes on average 2–3 hours and affords sweeping views of the whole island. A swim-and-hike option is also available and includes lunch on the beach at Anse L'Ivrogne and a water taxi to and from Soufrière. It is also possible to climb the seemingly vertical slopes of **Petit Piton**. However, you should be an experienced mountaineer and very fit, and should not attempt it alone or in wet weather; ask around Soufrière for a guide.

Several of the island's verdant river valleys are laced with walking trails, many of which culminate in a cool, inviting pool at the base of a waterfall. Two you can visit quite easily on your own or with a guide are the **Anse La Raye Waterfalls** and the **Saltibus waterfall and trail**.

If you do go hiking, bear in mind the tropical heat; wear light clothing and bring a hat, sunscreen and plenty of water. Sneakers are fine if you don't have walking shoes or boots, but know that paths can be extremely steep and are slippery after it rains.

Horseback riding

Horseback riding is a great way to see St Lucia, particularly its mountains or eastern coastline, where roads are poor and access by car is difficult. Most stables provide lessons as well as one- to four-hour rides, with transport to and from your hotel and possibly lunch included.

International Pony Club (☎ 452-8139 or ☎ 715-5689, ● www.international ponyclub.com) has three different trail rides to Cas-en-Bas Beach: an hour-and-a-quarter ride (US$40); a two-hour ride-and-swim trip (US$50); and a four-hour outing that includes a ride, a swim and a barbecue on the beach (US$70).

Similar one- and two-hour rides to Cas-en-Bas Beach as well as lessons are offered on Wednesdays and Thursdays through **Trim's Riding Stables** (☎ 450-8273).

Tennis and squash

Tennis is on offer at most hotels for as little as US$5 per hour. At the nine floodlit courts at St Lucia Racquet Club (☎ 450-0551), in *Club St Lucia by Splash* (see p.88), tennis is free for hotel guests and EC$25 per day for visitors; racquet rental is EC$20 per hour. The two courts at the *Royal St Lucian Hotel* on Reduit Beach (☎ 452-8351) are also open to the public for a fee, plus lessons are available. St Lucia Yacht Club in Rodney Bay (☎ 452-8350) will let non-members use its squash courts for EC$10 per hour and the *Jalousie Hilton Hotel* (☎ 459-7666) near Soufrière lets visitors use its courts for EC$25 per hour.

Golf

The St Lucia Golf and Country Club in Cap Estate (☎ 450-8523, ● www .stluciagolf.com) has the island's first and only eighteen-hole **public golf course** – a par 71 that's relatively challenging (note that it can get a little soggy during the rainy season). Green fees are US$95 for eighteen holes and US$70 for nine holes; golf club rental is US$20 and shoes are US$10. Lessons with the club pro run from US$40 for thirty minutes.

Gyms and spas

When it's time to work off all that Creole conch and rum punch, head for St Lucia's best **gym**, Sportivo at Rodney Heights (☎ 452-8899). Also on the island are: Body Inc, at the Gablewoods Mall (☎ 451-9744), owned by former Mr Universe and current politician and media magnate Rick Wayne; Mango Moon Total Fitness at Lunar Park, Vigie Marina (☎ 453-1934); The St Lucia Racquet Club (☎ 450-0551); and Doolittle's Gym at the Marigot Bay Beach Club in Marigot Bay (☎ 451-4974). Most are well-equipped with free weights, a good selection of brand-name units and machines such as treadmills; also, a variety of fitness classes are offered daily.

Entrance requires temporary membership – a rather hefty US$25 per day or US$80 per day for a family; rates are also available by the week or month. Many of the major hotels also have fitness rooms.

After you've worked your body to a pulp, you can let someone else work to soothe it. Numerous hotel **spas** offer a full range of beauty and health treatments including massages, facials, aromatherapy, hydrotherapy, mud wraps and manicures. In the Rodney Bay area, try the Royal Spa (☎ 452-9999) at the *Royal St Lucian* resort; the Cool Water Spa (☎ 452-8060) at the *Bay Gardens Inn*, the Village Inn and Spa (☎ 458-3300); the Oasis (☎ 457-7852) at the *Body Holiday at LeSport* in Cap Estate; or Serenity Spa (☎ 456-9585) at *Windjammer Landing* at Labrelotte Bay. In southern St Lucia, the Kai Belte Spa (☎ 459-7000) at *Anse Chastanet Resort* or the Ti Kai Pose Spa (☎ 459-7323) at the *Ladera Resort* will pamper your skin and muscles in lovely surroundings. Prices are on a par with European and North American spas.

Festivals and events

Though the biggest events, the Jazz Festival and Carnival, take place in May and July respectively, the roster of enjoyable celebrations spans the entire calendar year. As well, in Spring 2007 St Lucia will be one of eight hosts for the Cricket World Cup.

Late January

Nobel Laureate Week St Lucia celebrates its two Nobel laureates – Arthur Lewis for Economics and Derek Walcott for Literature – in the last week of January with public lectures on cerebral topics held in Castries.

February 22

Independence Day Political speeches and parades commemorate St Lucia's independence, which it gained in 1979.

Late March

Festival of Comedy ☎ 452-5005, ✉ www.slunatrust.org. This annual fundraiser held by the St Lucia National Trust at Pigeon Island features performances by local comedians, political satirists and storytellers. Visitors are welcome, though some plays may be in difficult-to-understand patois.

April

International Earth Day ☎ 452-5005, ✉ www.slunatrust.org. The day begins with a pre-dawn climb to Fort Rodney on Pigeon Island to watch buglers from the police band regale the rising sun.

May

St Lucia Jazz Festival ✉ www .stluciajazz.org. Venues in Castries, Pigeon Island and elsewhere host this four-day

Public holidays

January 1 New Year's Day
February 22 Independence Day
March/April Good Friday & Easter Monday
May 1 Labour Day
Seventh Monday after Easter Whit Monday
First Monday in August Emancipation Day
October Thanksgiving Day (first Monday in October)
December 13 National Day
December 25 Christmas Day
December 26 Boxing Day
Travellers should note that on public holidays most government offices, visitor information kiosks and shops are closed, while the majority of tourist attractions remain open.

event in early or mid-May. Big names are drawn from around the world to the increasingly popular open-air festival, so book accommodation far in advance if you plan to attend. Tickets average US$35 per person, per performance, or you can buy a festival pass for $230.

June 29
The Feast of St Peter Also called the Fishermen's Feast Day, this event includes religious services and the blessing of fishing boats, which are decorated for the occasion. It's a particularly big deal in Dennery, which is a stronghold of the industry.

July
Carnival ⊛ www.luciancarnival.com. One of the true showcases of the island's culture, this Castries event includes a week of storytelling, calypso and folk dancing alongside the mêlée of parades, thumping soca music, revellers in sequinned bikinis and women vying for the title of Carnival Queen.

Late August
The Feast of St Rose De Lima This event is hosted by members of La Rose – one of two competing flower societies (the other being La Marguerite). Micoud is the focal point for the festivities, but island-wide

activities include religious services, flower shows, costume parades, balls, feasts and performances of traditional St Lucian song and dance.

October
La Marguerite The Feast of St Margaret Mary Alacoque is celebrated on October 17 with public festivities, though they're more low key than those hosted by the La Rose flower society in August.

Jounen Kwéyòl Entenasyonnal (International Creole Day) Creole culture is honoured through music, storytelling, dance and lots and lots of food. St Lucia marks the day with enthusiam, scheduling events in Castries and three other villages around the island, selected on a rotating basis.

November 22
St Cecilia's Day The patron saint of music is feted with performances of traditional folk tunes alongside more modern jazz and calypso.

December 13
The Feast of St Lucy Island-wide dancing, eating and games honour St Lucia's namesake. Christmas festivities also commence on this day with the Festival of Lights and a procession of lanterns and Creole carols.

Directory

Airlines American Airlines ☎454-6777/79 or 454-6795; American Eagle ☎452-1820/40 or 454-8186/8259, ⊛www .aa.com; Air Canada ☎454-6038 or ☎1-800-744-2472, ⊛www.aircanada .com; Air Caraibes ☎452-2348, ⊛www .aircaraibes.com; Air France ☎458-8282/8283, ⊛www.airfrance.com; British Airways ☎452-3951/7444, ⊛www.ba.com British Midland ☎454-8186/8258, ⊛www .flybmi.com; BWIA International ☎452-3778 or 1-800-538-2942 (reservations) or 454-5075/5234, ⊛www.bwee.com; Caribbean Star ☎453-2927 or 1-800-744-STAR, ⊛www.flycaribbeanstar.com; Delta ☎454-3119, ⊛www.delta.com; LIAT ☎452-3056/2348, ⊛www.liatairline.com; SunAir ☎450-8100 or 458-1132, ⊛www .sunairstlucia.com; US Airways ☎1-800-622-1015, ⊛www.usairways.com; Virgin Atlantic ☎1-800-744-7477 or 454-3610, ⊛www.virgin-atlantic.com.

Banks Castries: Bank of Nova Scotia (Scotiabank), William Peter Blvd and corner of High St/Chausee Rd; Bank of St Lucia, 1 Bridge St; First Caribbean International, Bridge Street and Gablewoods Mall, Sunny Acres; Royal Bank of Canada, William Peter Blvd; RBTT Bank Caribbean, Micoud Street and Gablewoods Mall, Sunny Acres. **Rodney Bay**: Bank of Nova Scotia (Scotiabank), Reduit Drive, First Caribbean International, Rodney Bay Marina; Royal Bank of Canada, Rodney Bay Marina. **Soufrière**: Bank of St Lucia, Bridge St; First Caribbean International, Bridge St. **Vieux Fort**: Bank of Nova Scotia (Scotiabank), New Dock Rd; Bank of St Lucia, Clarke Street; First Caribbean International, New Dock Road; RBTT Bank Caribbean, Gablewoods Mall South; Royal Bank of Canada, New Dock Rd.

Banking hours are generally Mon–Thurs 8am–3pm and Fri 8am–5pm. The Royal Bank of Canada, Rodney Bay Marina, is open Saturday mornings. Most banks also have ATMs.

Courier services In Castries, FedEx on Derek Walcott Square (☎452-1320), DHL on Manoel Street (☎453-1538) and UPS on Bridge Street (☎452-7211).

Customs You are allowed a duty-free quota of one litre of spirits or wine, 200 cigarettes, 50 cigars and 250g of tobacco on arrival in St Lucia. The first EC$250 in gifts brought in (which includes the spirits and tobacco, but not personal effects) is not subject to duty charges. For questions, call Customs ☎454-6509; for customs information regarding your country of origin, contact the proper local authorities.

Departure tax Departure tax is EC$54 (US$22) per person, payable at the airport, or EC$30 (US$12) if you are leaving by ferry. It's best to have the exact sum.

Embassies and consulates British High Commission, Frances Compton Building, Waterfront, Castries ☎452-2484; French Embassy, Clarke Avenue, Vigie, Castries ☎452-2462/5877. The US, Australia and Canada are represented in Bridgetown, Barbados: US Consulate ☎1-246/431-0225; Australian High Commission ☎1-809/435-2834; Canadian High Commission ☎1-246/429-3550.

Emergencies For police dial ☎999; for fire and ambulance dial ☎911.

Gay and lesbian St Lucia While direct animosity is unlikely, St Lucia is one of the more backward islands in the Caribbean in its approach to gay visitors. In general, you may feel more comfortable at smaller hotels and guesthouses. The gay travel website ⊛www.purpleroofs.com lists several hotels and guesthouses on St Lucia that explicitly extend a welcome to gay travellers.

Internet access Most hotels and guesthouses offer Internet access, and Internet cafes are sprouting up all over the island. In **Castries**, you can go to Carib Travel (☎452-2151) at 28 Micoud St or Unitel (☎451-3000/3010) at 26 Maryann Street. In **Rodney Bay**, an Internet café is attached to the Big Chef Steakhouse restaurant. In **Vieux Fort**, try Carib Travel (☎454-6450) on Clarke Street and The Reef restaurant and bar (☎454-3418) on Anse des Sables Beach. Costs are generally EC$10 for 30min.

Laundry Hotel laundries are expensive, charging as much as US$2–5 for short-sleeved shirts and US$3–6 for long pants or skirts. The self-service machines at U Wash N Dry on Darling Rd in Castries (☎451-7664) are less expensive. You can also drop off washing at So White Cleaners on Marie Therese St in Gros Islet (☎450-8808) or in the laundromat in Gablewoods Mall. In Vieux Fort, there's Fletcher's Dry Cleaning and Laundry Service, New Dock Rd (☎454-5936).

Measurements St Lucia is gradually switching from imperial to metric. Most road signs are in miles; petrol is sold by the litre; and fishermen weigh and sell their catch by the pound.

Medical assistance Castries: Victoria Hospital ☎453-7059; **Rodney Bay**: Rodney Bay Medical and Dental Centre ☎452-8621; **Vieux Fort**: St. Jude's Hospital ☎454-6041.

Pharmacies Castries: MC Drugstore, Bridge St (☎458-8147/8000) and Gablewoods Mall (☎458-8151/8000), Clarke's Drugstore, 6 Bridge St (☎452-2727); **Rodney Bay**: MC Drugstore, JQ Mall (☎458-8153/8000), Julian's Pharmacy at Julian's Supermarket (☎458-4992 or 459-0100); **Vieux Fort**: MC Drugstore, New Dock Road (☎458-8154/8155/8000), Julian's Pharmacy at Julian's Supermarket (☎454-5970).

Post All major towns and villages have a post office; the major ones in Anse La Raye, Castries, Dennery, Gros Islet, Micoud, Soufrière and Vieux Fort are open Monday to Friday between 8.15am and 4.30pm, while the smaller offices only open between 1pm and 5pm. The General Post Office on Bridge Street in Castries (☎452-5157) is the island's largest and has a philatelic bureau. Sending postcards and packages to the US, Canada or Europe costs less than EC$1.

Time St Lucia is on Atlantic Standard Time, four hours behind Greenwich Mean Time and one hour ahead of Eastern Standard Time. No seasonal adjustments are made.

Tipping and taxes Hotels add a ten percent service charge and an eight percent government tax on room charges, which may be included in the rates or added on to your final bill. Restaurants often add a ten percent service charge, though feel free to add a further tip. Taxi drivers have come to expect a ten to fifteen percent tip.

Visas All visitors to St. Lucia must carry a valid passport, except for citizens of OECS countries, who may enter with a driving licence or another piece of official photo identification. Citizens of the US, all British Commonwealth countries, Germany, Austria, France, Italy and Spain can enter St Lucia without a visa and stay for up to 42 days; longer stays must be arranged through the St Lucia Immigration Department (Bridge St, Castries, next to the Police Station, ☎456-3787; visa office open mornings only). All other nationals require a visa, obtainable in their country of origin prior to travel. To obtain a visa extension for up to three weeks, you will need to present two passport photos, EC$100 and leave your passport at the Immigration Department office for 48 hours for processing.

Weddings To get married in St Lucia, you must bring the originals of your passport and birth certificate, as well as appropriate documentation if either partner has been divorced or is a widow/widower. Once on St Lucia, you must appoint a local solicitor to apply for a marriage license, which will be issued after you have been on the island for two days; the application takes two business days to process. Total fees amount to around US$300. Most hotels offer wedding packages; alternatively, try Dreamy Weddings and Tours, Castries (☎452-6473, ⊛www.dreamyweddings.com).

Travel store

ROUGH GUIDES Complete Listing

Available from all good bookstores   D: Rough Guide DIRECTIONS

Kenya
Marrakesh **D**
Morocco
South Africa,
    Lesotho &
    Swaziland
Syria
Tanzania
Tunisia
West Africa
Zanzibar

Travel Specials
First-Time
    Around the
    World
First-Time Asia
First-Time
    Europe
First-Time Latin
    America
Travel Online
Travel Health
Travel Survival
Walks in London
    & SE England
Women Travel

Maps
Algarve
Amsterdam
Andalucia &
    Costa del Sol
Argentina
Athens
Australia
Barcelona
Berlin
Boston
Brittany
Brussels
California
Chicago
Corsica
Costa Rica &
    Panama
Crete
Croatia
Cuba
Cyprus
Czech Republic
Dominican
    Republic
Dubai & UAE
Dublin
Egypt
Florence & Siena
Florida

France
Frankfurt
Germany
Greece
Guatemala &
    Belize
Hong Kong
Iceland
Ireland
Kenya &
    Northern
    Tanzania
Lisbon
London
Los Angeles
Madrid
Mallorca
Malaysia
Marrakesh
Mexico
Miami & Key
    West
Morocco
New England
New York City
New Zealand
Northern Spain
Paris
Peru
Portugal
Prague
The Pyrenees
Rome
San Francisco
Sicily
South Africa
South India
Spain & Portugal
Sri Lanka
Tenerife
Thailand
Toronto
Trinidad &
    Tobago
Tuscany
Venice
Vietnam, Laos &
    Cambodia
Washington DC
Yucatán
    Peninsula

**Dictionary
Phrasebooks**
Croatian
Czech
Dutch
Egyptian Arabic

French
German
Greek
Hindi & Urdu
Italian
Japanese
Latin American
    Spanish
Mandarin
    Chinese
Mexican Spanish
Polish
Portuguese
Russian
Spanish
Swahili
Thai
Turkish
Vietnamese

Computers
Blogging
iPods, iTunes &
    music online
The Internet
Macs & OS X
PCs and Windows
Playstation
    Portable
Website Directory

Film & TV
American
    Independent
    Film
British Cult
    Comedy
Chick Flicks
Comedy Movies
Cult Movies
Gangster Movies
Horror Movies
James Bond
Kids' Movies
Sci-Fi Movies
Westerns

Lifestyle
eBay
Ethical Shopping
Babies
Pregnancy
    & Birth

Music Guides
The Beatles
Bob Dylan
Classical Music
Elvis
Frank Sinatra
Heavy Metal
Hip-Hop
Jazz
Book of Playlists
Opera
Pink Floyd
Punk
Reggae
Rock
The Rolling
    Stones
Soul and R&B
World Music
    (2 vols)

Popular Culture
Books for
    Teenagers
Children's Books,
    0-5
Children's Books,
    5-11
Conspiracy
    Theories
Cult Fiction
The Da Vinci
    Code
Lord of the Rings
Shakespeare
Superheroes
Unexplained
    Phenomena

Sport
Arsenal 11s
Celtic 11s
Chelsea 11s
Liverpool 11s
Man United 11s
Newcastle 11s
Rangers 11s
Tottenham 11s
Poker

Science
Climate Change
The Universe
Weather

For more information go to www.roughguides.com

ROUGH
GUIDES

Listen Up!

"You may be used to the Rough Guide series being comprehensive, but nothing will prepare you for the exhaustive Rough Guide to World Music . . . one of our books of the year."

Sunday Times, London

Rough Guide Music Titles

Bob Dylan • The Beatles • Classical Music
Elvis • Frank Sinatra • Heavy Metal • Hip-Hop
iPods, iTunes & music online • Jazz
Book of Playlists • Opera • Pink Floyd • Punk
Reggae • Rock • The Rolling Stones
Soul and R&B • World Music Vol 1 & 2

BROADEN YOUR HORIZONS

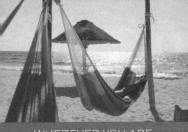

WHEREVER YOU ARE,

WHEREVER YOU'RE GOING,

WE'VE GOT YOU COVERED!

Rough Guides Travel Insurance

Visit our website at www.roughguides.com/insurance or call:

- UK: 0800 083 9507
- Spain: 900 997 149
- Australia: 1300 669 999
- New Zealand: 0800 55 99 11
- Worldwide: +44 870 890 2843
- USA, call toll free on: 1 800 749 4922

Please quote our ref: **Rough Guides books**

Cover for over 46 different nationalities and available in 4 different languages.

Small print & Index

SMALL PRINT

A Rough Guide to Rough Guides

In 1981, Mark Ellingham, a recent graduate in English from Bristol University, was travelling in Greece on a tiny budget and couldn't find the right guidebook. With a group of friends he wrote his own guide, combining a contemporary, journalistic style with a practical approach to travellers' needs. That first Rough Guide was a student scheme that became a publishing phenomenon. Today, Rough Guides include recommendations from shoestring to luxury and cover hundreds of destinations around the globe, including almost every country in the Americas and Europe, more than half of Africa and most of Asia and Australasia. Millions of readers relish Rough Guides' wit and inquisitiveness as much as they enthusiastic, critical approach and value-for-money ethos. The guides' ever-growing team of authors and photographers is spread all over the world.

In the early 1990s, Rough Guides branched out of travel, with the publication of Rough Guides to World Music, Classical Music and the Internet. All three have become benchmark titles in their fields, spearheading the publication of a range of more than 350 titles under the Rough Guide name, including phrasebooks, waterproof maps, music guides from Opera to Heavy Metal, reference works as diverse as Conspiracy Theories and Shakespeare, and popular culture books from iPods to Poker. Rough Guides also produce a series of more than 120 World Music CDs in partnership with World Music Network.

Visit www.roughguides.com to see our latest publications.

Rough Guide travel images are available for commercial licensing at www.roughguidespictures.com

Publishing information

This first edition published September 2006 by **Rough Guides Ltd**, 80 Strand, London WC2R 0RL. 345 Hudson St, 4th Floor, New York, NY 10014, USA.

Distributed by the Penguin Group
Penguin Books Ltd, 80 Strand, London WC2R 0RL
Penguin Group (USA), 375 Hudson Street, NY 10014, USA
14 Local Shopping Centre, Panchsheel Park, New Delhi 110017, India
Penguin Group (Australia), 250 Camberwell Road, Camberwell, Victoria 3124, Australia
Penguin Group (Canada), 10 Alcorn Avenue, Toronto, ON M4V 1E4, Canada
Penguin Group (New Zealand), Cnr Rosedale and Airborne Roads, Albany, Auckland, New Zealand
Typeset in Bembo and Helvetica to an original design by Henry Iles.

Printed and bound in China
© Rough Guides 2006

No part of this book may be reproduced in any form without permission from the publisher except for the quotation of brief passages in reviews.
176pp includes index

A catalogue record for this book is available from the British Library

ISBN 13: 978-1-84353-665-9

ISBN 10: 1-84353-665-X

The publishers and authors have done their best to ensure the accuracy and currency of all the information in St Lucia DIRECTIONS, however, they can accept no responsibility for any loss, injury, or inconvenience sustained by any traveller as a result of information or advice contained in the guide.

1 3 5 7 9 8 6 4 2

Help us update

We've gone to a lot of effort to ensure that the first edition of St Lucia DIRECTIONS is accurate and up-to-date. However, things change – places get "discovered", opening hours are notoriously fickle, restaurants and rooms raise prices or lower standards. If you feel we've got it wrong or left something out, we'd like to know, and if you can remember the address, the price, the phone number, so much the better.

We'll credit all contributions, and send a copy of the next edition (or any other DIRECTIONS guide or Rough Guide if you prefer) for the best letters. Everyone who writes to us and isn't already a subscriber will receive a copy of our full-colour thrice-yearly newsletter. Please mark letters: "St Lucia DIRECTIONS Update" and send to: Rough Guides, 80 Strand, London WC2R 0RL, or Rough Guides, 4th Floor, 345 Hudson St, New York, NY 10014. Or send an email to mail@roughguides.com

Have your questions answered and tell others about your trip at www.roughguides.atinfopop.com.

Rough Guide credits

Text editor: Amy Hegarty
Layout: Jessica Subramanian
Photography: Roger Mapp
Cartography: Ed Wright

Picture editor: Harriet Mills
Proofreader: Stewart J. Wild
Production: Katherine Owers
Cover design: Chloë Roberts

SMALL PRINT

The authors

Natalie Folster is from New Brunswick, Canada, and has lived, worked and travelled in Canada, the United States, Africa, Europe and parts of the Caribbean.

Karl Luntta is the author of guides to Jamaica, the Virgin Islands and Lesser Antilles, and has written on the islands for numerous publications. He has published short fiction in *International Quarterly*, *Baltimore Review* and *North Atlantic Review*, as well as the novel *Know it by Heart*.

Acknowledgements

Natalie would like to thank Verena Lawaetz for a wealth of detailed information, the nameless truckload of guys who lifted her car out of a ditch and back onto the road on a dark, rainy night in Soufrière and Amy Hegarty for her patience, skill and diligence in editing this guide.

Photo credits

All images © Rough Guides except the following:

p.10 Visitors walking through rainforest © St Lucia Tourist Board
p.11 Choc Beach © St Lucia Tourist Board
p.11 Queen Angelfish, Caribbean © Constantinos Petrinos/Naturepl.com
p.13 Reduit Beach © Ian Cumming/Axiom
p.14 Piton Flore trail © Chris Huxley
p.14 Saltibus waterfall near Balenbouche Estate © Balenbouche Estate/Francois Gilbert
p.16 Diving over coral reef at Anse Chastanet © M. Timothy O'Keefe/Alamy
p.16 Deep-sea fishing off St Lucia © Chris Huxley
p.17 Sailing activities at Reduit Beach © James Davis Photography/Alamy
p.17 Sea kayaking at Anse Mamin © Chris Huxley
p.18 Fond Doux Estate © Chris Huxley
p.19 La Sikwi Sugar Mill © Richard Cummins/SuperStock
p.19 Balenbouche Estate sugar mill © Balenbouche Estate/Chris Huxley
p.21 Fruit and vegetable market, Soufriere © Yadid Levy/Alamy
p.23 Treehouse Restaurant, Anse Chastanet © Anse Chastanet Resort
p.29 Ti Kaye Village © Danielle Devaux/Ti Kaye Village
p.29 Balenbouche Estate © Balenbouche Estate/Chris Huxley

p.30 Pottery at La Pointe Caribe © Chris Huxley
p.31 Creole music at Jounen Kwéyòl Entenasyonnal © Chris Huxley
p.32 Stonefield Estate © St Lucia Tourist Board
p.32 Pigeon Island ruins © St Lucia Tourist Board
p.36 Gros Piton aerial view © St Lucia Tourist Board
p.38 Mountain biking © Chris Huxley
p.42 Leatherback turtle © Doug Perrine/Naturepl.com
p.43 Fer de lance snake © blickwinkel/Alamy
p.43 St Lucia Parrot © Dave Watts/Naturepl.com
p.43 Frigate bird © Chris Huxley
p.44 Festival of Lights, Derek Walcott Square, Castries © Chris Huxley
p.44 La Rose festival © Chris Huxley
p.45 Carnvial, St Lucia © AM Corporation/Alamy
p.45 Jounen Kwéyòl Entenasyonnal © Chris Huxley
p.47 Compton Corsini, Anse La Raye © Danita Delimont/Alamy
p.47 St Lucia Jazz Festival © St Lucia Tourist Board
p.60 Almond Morgan Bay Resort © Almond Morgan Bay Resort
p.116 Church, Choiseul © Andre Jenny/Alamy
p.139 Des Cartiers Rainforest Trail © M. Timothy O'Keefe/Alamy
p.141 Piton Flore trail steps © Chris Huxley

Selected images from our guidebooks are available for licensing from:
ROUGHGUIDESPICTURES.COM

Index

Maps are marked in colour